How to Overcome Pet Loss, Grief & Begin Healing

A Simple Yet Powerful step-by-step Guide to Coping, Finding Comfort, and Honoring Your Beloved Companion Without Feeling Stuck in Grief

Andre St Pierre

ISBN (Paperback): 978-1-997535-00-3

ISBN (Hardcover): 978-1-997535-01-0

ISBN (eBook): 978-1-997535-02-7

To my children Isabelle, Vivienne and Xavier and to my beloved Erin, I love you and thank you for your support. You mean the world to me.

To my beautiful dogs Snowball (RIP), Bear (RIP) and Teddy - our time together is never enough and your paw prints are forever etched in our hearts.

"Dogs come into our lives to teach us about love, they depart to teach us about loss."

Table Of Contents

A Special Thank You

Knowing and understanding you are going through a challenging time and as a way of saying thanks for your purchase, I'm offering an early copy of the book ***Wagging Tails & Timeless Tales: 9 Touching Short Stories that Capture the Magic of Dogs – Through Joy, Loss and a Lifetime of Love*** for **FREE** to my readers.

To get instant access just go to https://pawsitivepuppybooks.com/Puppy-Opt-in-Page or scan the QR Code below:

Inside the book of short stories, you will discover:

🐾 **Nine heartwarming stories**

🐾 **Tales of unconditional love**

🐾 **The bittersweet reality of saying goodbye**

🐾 **How dogs help us heal**

The book you are about to read will help you to start healing and, as part of that process, this book of short stories will make you **laugh, cry and smile** so please grab a copy of the free book today.

Why This Book Will Help You Heal

"What we have once enjoyed we can never lose. All that we love deeply becomes a part of us."
— Helen Keller

You're Not Alone in Your Grief

If you're reading this, chances are you've lost a beloved companion—your dog who greeted you at the door every evening, your cat who curled up next to you after a long day, or maybe even a rabbit, bird, or another cherished pet who left an imprint on your soul. And right now, your heart aches in a way that feels impossible to put into words.

I want to start by saying something that too many people hesitate to say out loud: **pet loss is real loss.** The grief you feel is not "just" about an animal—it's about losing a best friend, a source of unconditional love, and a daily presence that made life brighter. It's about the empty spaces, the routines now broken, the silence where joyful sounds once filled the air.

Yet, despite the depth of this loss, many well-meaning people around you might not fully understand. Society tends to minimize pet loss—offering dismissive comments like, "It was just a pet" or "You can always get another one." But you know better. Your bond was unique, irreplaceable. And if you feel stuck in your grief, unsure how to move forward without leaving them behind, this book is here to help.

My Story: The Search for Healing

I've been where you are now. I've sat in the quiet of an empty house, waiting to hear the familiar click of paws on the floor or the soft sigh of a companion curling up beside me. I've had moments where the weight of loss made it hard to breathe. I remember feeling like I had no right to grieve this deeply—like I had to hide my pain because the world didn't see it as "serious" enough.

For a long time, I struggled to figure out how to heal. I read everything I could find on grief—some books helped, others didn't. I learned through trial and error what brought me comfort, what kept me stuck, and what ultimately allowed me to move forward without feeling like I was letting go.

This journey led me to explore both the emotional and psychological sides of grief. I sought out experts in pet loss, delved into research on how our brains process loss, and spoke to countless people who had walked this same painful path. What I found was a **step-by-step approach to healing**—one that is both **science-backed and deeply compassionate**. One that honors the love you shared while helping you regain your sense of peace.

A Path Forward—Together

If you're struggling with pet loss, this book is here to walk beside you. It won't tell you to "move on" or "get over it." Instead, it will help you:

☑ **Understand** why pet loss grief is so profound and valid.

☑ **Work through** the pain without guilt, regret, or feeling stuck.

☑ **Honor** your pet in a way that keeps their memory alive while allowing you to heal.

☑ **Find comfort** in the shared experiences of others who have grieved before you.

Most importantly, this book will remind you that **you are not alone**. Grief is heavy, but you don't have to carry it by yourself.

So take a deep breath. You've already taken the first step by picking up this book. **Turn the page, and let's begin your journey toward healing together.**

CHAPTER 1

Understanding Your Grief— Why It Feels So Overwhelming

"Grief is the price we pay for love."
— Queen Elizabeth II

When we lose a pet, the grief can feel all-consuming. It can hit us in ways we never expected, leaving us raw, unmoored, and struggling to find solid ground. Some people may not understand. They may think, *It was just a pet.* But you know better. Your pet was never *just* anything. They were your companion, your confidant, your source of comfort and unconditional love.

The depth of your grief is a reflection of the depth of your bond. And that bond wasn't just emotional—it was biological. Science confirms what every pet lover already knows in their heart: our connection with animals is deeply ingrained in us, and when they leave, they take a piece of us with them. To understand why this loss is so overwhelming, we need to look at what makes our bond with pets so profound in the first place.

Section 1: The Science of Grief

Why We Bond So Deeply with Pets

If you've ever looked into your pet's eyes and felt an instant wave of love, there's a scientific reason for that. It's called **oxytocin**, often known as the *love hormone*. It's the same chemical that strengthens bonds between parents and children, romantic partners, and close friends. When you pet your dog, cuddle your cat, or even just make eye contact with them, your brain releases oxytocin, reinforcing feelings of attachment, trust, and deep connection.

But what makes this bond with pets even more unique is its **purity**. Human relationships are complex—sometimes messy, sometimes conditional. But with pets, love is simple. There's no judgment, no hidden agendas. Whether you've had a bad day, made mistakes, or feel completely unlovable, your pet sees you the same way: as their person, their safe place, their whole world.

This is why losing them is so devastating. It's not just about missing their presence—it's about losing that steady, unwavering source of love and acceptance.

The Role of Pets in Emotional Regulation and Stress Relief

For many people, pets aren't just companions—they're a lifeline. Studies have shown that interacting with animals can **reduce stress, lower blood pressure, and even decrease symptoms of anxiety and depression**. When you're feeling overwhelmed, a pet's presence can be grounding. The simple act of stroking their fur, hearing their breathing, or feeling their warmth beside you can provide an immediate sense of calm.

This isn't just emotional—it's physiological. Petting an animal has been proven to lower **cortisol**, the hormone associated with stress, while increasing **serotonin and dopamine**, the chemicals that help regulate mood. In other words, your pet was literally helping you feel better, both mentally and physically, on a daily basis.

Think about how many times your pet has comforted you without a single word. Maybe they nudged your hand when they sensed you were sad. Maybe they sat quietly by your side when you were grieving something else. Maybe they made you laugh on days when nothing else could.

Now that they're gone, it's not just their physical presence that's missing—it's the way they helped you navigate life's ups and downs. It's no wonder their absence leaves such a profound void.

Why Losing a Pet Creates a Profound Emotional Void

Grief over a pet is so powerful because it isn't just about losing *one* thing. It's about losing **many** things all at once:

- Your **daily routine**—the morning walks, the feeding schedule, the greetings at the door.
- Your **sense of security**—the quiet companionship, the feeling that you're never truly alone.

- Your **emotional support**—the nonverbal comfort, the unconditional presence.

- Your **identity as a pet parent**—the role you played in caring for them, protecting them, loving them.

For many, pets are the first ones we see in the morning and the last ones we say goodnight to. They are woven into the fabric of our everyday lives in ways we don't fully realize until they're gone. And when they leave, the silence is deafening. The space they filled is suddenly, achingly empty.

This is why pet loss can feel just as, if not more, intense than losing a human loved one. **It's not just the loss of an animal—it's the loss of a relationship that was deeply entwined with your sense of comfort, stability, and love.**

But here's the most important thing to remember: **this grief is real, and it matters.**

If you feel like the world doesn't understand, know that you are not alone. If you feel like you're struggling to move forward, know that there is no "right" way to grieve. And if you feel like the pain is too much to bear, know that you will find a way to carry this love forward, even through the sorrow.

Right now, the loss may feel overwhelming, but in time, healing will come—not by forgetting, but by finding new ways to honor the bond that will always be a part of you.

How Grief Affects the Brain and Body

> *"Grief never ends... But it changes. It's a passage, not a place to stay. Grief is not a sign of weakness, nor a lack of faith... It is the price of love."*
> *— Unknown*

Grief isn't just an emotional experience—it's a full-body response. If you feel physically exhausted, mentally foggy, or even sick in the aftermath of losing your pet, there's a reason for that.

*Losing a beloved companion isn't just about missing them; it's about your brain and body adjusting to a world without them. Scientists have studied grief in depth and found that it alters **brain function, hormone levels, and even immune response**. When you lose a pet, the effects of that grief can be felt in every part of your being— from your thoughts to your heart rate to the very way you move through your day.*

*If you've been feeling like something is wrong with you because your body is reacting so intensely to this loss, I want you to know: **this is normal. You are not broken. This is how grief works.***

The Neurological Impact of Grief

Grief isn't just emotional—it's neurological. When we bond with a pet, they become a part of our daily patterns, our brain's expectations, our sense of normalcy. Their absence disrupts this in profound ways.

*Neurologists have found that grief activates the **same parts of the brain as physical pain**—which explains why it can feel like your chest is tight, your stomach is in knots, or you can't catch your breath. The brain perceives deep loss as a kind of trauma, triggering the same fight-or-flight response you might experience in a crisis.*

*Even more than that, grief can disrupt the brain's **default mode network (DMN)**—the part of our mind that controls memory, emotions, and identity. This is why, in the immediate aftermath of loss, people often experience:*

- ***Forgetfulness*** *– Walking into a room and not remembering why you're there.*

- ***Difficulty concentrating*** *– Simple tasks feel mentally exhausting.*

- ***Disorientation*** *– Losing track of time or feeling detached from reality.*

Your brain is struggling to reconcile two conflicting realities: the expectation that your pet should be there, and the painful truth that they're not. This is why it's so common to hear their footsteps or see their shape out of the corner of your eye, only to remember they're gone. Your brain is still wired for their presence.

And while this can feel disorienting, it's also proof of just how deeply they were woven into your life.

Physical Symptoms of Pet Loss Grief

*People often think of grief as something emotional—but it's just as physical as it is mental. Studies have shown that grief can lead to **a weakened immune system,***

9

increased inflammation, and even changes in heart function.

Some of the most common physical symptoms of pet loss grief include:

- **Exhaustion** – *Even if you're sleeping, you might wake up feeling drained.*

- **Loss of appetite or nausea** – *Grief disrupts digestion, often leading to stomach issues.*

- **Tightness in the chest** – *This is sometimes called "heartache" for a reason.*

- **Headaches or migraines** – *The emotional stress of loss can trigger physical pain.*

- **Body aches** – *Grief-related stress can lead to muscle tension and soreness.*

- **Shortness of breath or panic attacks** – *Anxiety often accompanies deep grief.*

*One of the most surprising things about grief is how **deeply tiring** it is. Even if you aren't crying all day, your body is **processing an emotional overload**. This takes energy. Be kind to yourself. Listen to your body. Allow yourself to rest when you need it.*

And if your grief feels overwhelming—so much so that it's interfering with your ability to eat, sleep, or function for an extended period—it's important to reach out for support. You don't have to go through this alone.

Why Grief Can Feel Like Depression—But Isn't Always the Same

*One of the hardest parts of grieving a pet is the **emotional weight** it carries. Many people describe feeling hollow, directionless, or even numb. Others experience waves of sadness that feel like they may never end.*

*In many ways, grief mimics depression—but they aren't always the same thing. **Grief is a natural response to loss, while depression is a prolonged mental health condition that can persist even in the absence of loss.***

The key differences between grief and depression are:

1. ***Grief comes in waves, while depression feels constant.***
    - *With grief, some moments bring deep sadness, while others bring relief, memories, or even laughter.*
    - *With depression, the low mood doesn't lift, even in lighter moments.*
2. ***Grief allows for connection, while depression isolates.***
    - *People grieving may still feel comforted by family, friends, or memories of their pet.*
    - *Depression, on the other hand, often makes people feel disconnected from everything, including loved ones.*

3. *Grief eventually softens, while depression lingers.*

- ○ *Over time, grief slowly integrates into life in a way that allows for joy to return.*

- ○ *Depression, if untreated, continues to weigh down daily life indefinitely.*

That said, **grief can turn into depression***, especially if it's prolonged, complicated, or combined with other major life stressors. If your grief* **isn't easing over time** *or feels like it's pulling you into darkness,* **seeking professional support is not a sign of weakness— it's a way to help yourself heal.**

A Story of Love and Loss: Saying Goodbye to Max

I still remember the last time I saw Max. His graying muzzle rested gently on my knee, his deep brown eyes looking up at me with the same trust and love they had since the day I brought him home. He had always been my shadow, following me from room to room, never letting me out of his sight. But on that day, he was too tired to get up.

Max had been with me for thirteen years—through breakups, job changes, moves to new cities. He had been the one constant in my life, the steady heartbeat in a world that often felt unpredictable. He had this way of knowing when I was upset, pressing his head against my leg, as if to say, *I'm here. It's okay.*

And now, here we were. I sat beside him on the floor, my hand resting on his fur, trying to memorize the rise and fall of his breathing. The vet had gently explained that his heart was failing, that he was in pain, and that I had a choice to make. A choice that felt impossible.

I had prepared myself for this moment—or at least I thought I had. I had read about pet loss, told myself that I would be strong, that I wouldn't let him suffer just because I wasn't ready to say goodbye. But when the moment came, I felt like a child again, lost and desperate, clinging to the hope that maybe, just maybe, he would wake up tomorrow and be okay.

When it was time, I whispered everything I needed him to know. That he was the best dog. That he had given me more love than I ever thought possible. That I was sorry if I ever failed him. That I would carry him in my heart forever.

And then, just like that, he was gone.

In the days that followed, the house felt unbearably quiet. I kept expecting to hear the jingle of his collar, to feel his nose nudging my hand for attention. I found myself still pouring his food in the morning out of habit, only to stare at the bowl, my stomach twisting with grief.

People around me tried to be kind, but not all of them understood. "You can always get another dog," some said. As if another soul could replace the one I had lost. As if love worked that way.

Grief came in waves. Some days, I was okay. Other days, I would find his old leash tucked in a drawer and break down all over again. I wondered if I had done the right thing, if I had let him go too soon or too late. The guilt, the what-ifs, they weighed on me.

But slowly, I started to realize that grief wasn't something to *get over*. It was something to *carry differently*. It was proof of how much he had meant to me, how deeply he had been woven into my life. I started talking about him more, not just in sadness, but in gratitude. I looked at pictures, laughed at the ridiculous things he used to do—like the time he stole an entire Thanksgiving turkey off the counter and ran victorious into the backyard.

And little by little, the pain softened.

Max wasn't *gone*—not really. His love was still here, in the way I carried myself, in the way I looked at other dogs with warmth, in the way I had learned to love deeper because of him.

That's what I hold onto now. Not just the sorrow of losing him, but the love that made saying goodbye so hard in the first place.

Because grief, at its core, is love that has nowhere to go. And I choose to believe that love never truly leaves us.

Final Thoughts

The way grief affects the brain and body explains why losing a pet feels so overwhelming. Your mind, your heart, and even your physical body are all processing the loss in ways that can be exhausting, disorienting, and even painful.

*But what I want you to remember is this: **you are not alone in this experience.** What you're feeling— mentally, physically, and emotionally—is a natural part of loving deeply and losing something precious.*

Grief is love in another form. And in time, the pain you feel now will soften—not because you've forgotten, but because love finds new ways to live on.

For now, be patient with yourself. Give yourself grace. And when you're ready, we'll take the next step forward together.

The Non-Linear Nature of Grief

"Grief is like the ocean; it comes in waves, ebbing and flowing. Sometimes the water is calm, sometimes it is overwhelming. All we can do is learn to swim." — Vicki Harrison

One day, you might feel like you're finally finding your footing again. The next, you're in tears because you found an old toy under the couch or heard a sound that made you think, just for a second, that your pet was still there. This is how grief works—it doesn't move in a straight line.

Yet, so many of us expect it to. We think that if we just give it time, we'll get through it step by step until one day, it's *gone*. But grief doesn't follow a neat timeline. It isn't something you "finish." Instead, it weaves itself into your life in unpredictable ways, sometimes resurfacing when you least expect it.

If you've been wondering why you're still breaking down months later, why you feel okay one moment and completely lost the next, know this: **this is normal. This is grief.**

The Myth of the "5 Stages" of Grief

Many of us have heard of the **five stages of grief**: denial, anger, bargaining, depression, and acceptance. This model, introduced by psychiatrist Elisabeth Kübler-Ross, was originally meant to describe the emotions of terminally ill patients facing their own mortality. Over time, people began applying it to all forms of loss—including pet loss.

But the problem with this model is that it makes grief sound like a checklist. Like if you just make it to "acceptance," you're done grieving. **That's not how grief works.**

In reality, grief is messy. You might feel acceptance one day, then return to anger the next. You might skip stages altogether or cycle through them multiple times. You might not experience anger at all, but instead feel overwhelming guilt, or numbness, or deep sadness that comes and goes without warning.

There is no "right" way to grieve. There is no order, no step-by-step process. And that means **there's no way to do it wrong.**

How Everyone Experiences Grief Differently

Grief is as unique as the bond you shared with your pet. No two losses feel the same, because no two relationships are the same.

Some people grieve quietly, keeping their emotions close, while others need to talk about their loss with anyone who will listen. Some people find comfort in getting another pet, while others can't bear the thought of it for years. Some cry every day. Some don't cry at all but feel the pain in different ways—through exhaustion, through lack of motivation, through a sense of emptiness they can't put into words.

However you are grieving right now, it is valid. If your grief feels different from what others expect, that doesn't mean you're grieving *wrong*. It just means you're grieving *your way*.

One of the hardest parts of losing a pet is that there is no set roadmap for healing. There is no way to know when the waves of grief will lessen or when the pain will become easier to bear. But if there's one thing I can tell you, it's this: **you won't always feel the way you do right now.**

Grief may never fully leave, but it will change. The love you had for your pet will remain, but the rawness of the loss will soften. The moments of sorrow will, over time, be met with moments of warmth—memories that make you smile instead of break.

For now, let yourself grieve in the way that feels right for you. Take the time you need. And when the waves hit hard, remember—you are not alone in this.

Disenfranchised Grief—When Others Don't Understand

> *"Grief, no matter who or what it is for, deserves to be honored." — Unknown*

One of the hardest parts of losing a pet isn't just the pain of the loss itself—it's the way the world responds to it. Or rather, the way it *doesn't*.

When you lose a human loved one, there are rituals. There are condolences, sympathy cards, understanding nods from people who recognize the weight of your loss. But when you lose a pet, those same responses don't always come. Instead, you might hear:

- *"It was just a dog."*
- *"You can always get another one."*
- *"At least it wasn't a person."*

These words can feel like a slap in the face. They minimize something that, to you, is massive. And sometimes, that dismissal can make you question your own emotions. *Am I overreacting? Should I be handling this better?*

Let me be clear: **your grief is real, and it matters.** Just because society doesn't always acknowledge pet loss the same way it does human loss doesn't mean your pain is any less valid.

Why Society Minimizes Pet Loss

The world often places pets in a different category than humans. They're seen as companions, as *extras* in our lives—important, yes, but not *essential*. Many people don't understand that for those of us who love our pets like family, their loss feels just as devastating as losing a person.

Some people simply haven't formed the kind of deep, emotional bond with an animal that you have. They don't know what it's like to have a pet who was more than a pet—who was a best friend, a confidant, a daily presence in their life. Because they haven't felt that connection, they struggle to comprehend the depth of the grief.

Others may recognize that pet loss is hard but believe that since pets have shorter lifespans, we should somehow be "prepared" for their passing. As if knowing a goodbye is inevitable ever makes it *easier*.

And then there are those who just don't know what to say. Instead of offering the comfort you need, they default to *fixing*—suggesting you get another pet or reminding you of how "good of a life" your pet had. They mean well, but their words don't always land the way they intend.

How to Validate Your Own Grief

The most important thing you can do right now is **give yourself permission to grieve.** You don't need society's validation to know that your loss is significant. **You already know it in your heart.**

Your pet was real. Your love for them was real. And so, your grief is real.

If you find yourself questioning whether your emotions are "too much," remind yourself:

- **Loss is loss.** There is no rule about who or what you're allowed to grieve.

- **Love doesn't have hierarchy.** Losing a pet is just as worthy of mourning as losing a human.

- **Your grief is personal.** No one else gets to define it for you.

Grief is not about logic. It's not about whether others think your pain is justified. It's about the fact that you loved deeply, and now, you're hurting. That alone makes your grief valid.

Strategies to Respond to Dismissive Comments

While some people will offer genuine support, others might not understand the weight of your loss. When that happens, you have a few choices.

1. Educate Gently

Some people simply don't realize how dismissive their words are. If you feel up to it, you can respond in a way that helps them understand.

- **"I know some people don't see it this way, but my pet was family to me. This loss is really painful."**

- **"Losing my pet has been one of the hardest things I've ever gone through. They were a huge part of my life."**

Sometimes, a little explanation can open someone's eyes to how deeply this loss is affecting you.

2. Set Boundaries

Not everyone deserves an explanation. If someone repeatedly dismisses your grief or makes you feel worse, it's okay to set a boundary.

- **"I appreciate your perspective, but this is really painful for me. I'd rather not talk about it if it's not going to be taken seriously."**
- **"I need support right now, not advice."**

You don't owe anyone justification for your grief. If someone isn't supportive, you have the right to step away.

3. Find Support in the Right Places

If the people around you aren't validating your grief, seek out those who will. There are **pet loss support groups, online communities, and even therapists** who specialize in animal-related grief. Surrounding yourself with people who understand can make all the difference.

Final Thoughts

Disenfranchised grief—the kind that isn't widely acknowledged—can feel isolating. But just because others may not see your loss the way you do **doesn't mean it isn't real**.

Grief is love in another form. And the love you had for your pet? It was big, and deep, and beautiful. That kind of love doesn't disappear overnight.

So grieve how you need to grieve. Mourn as fully as you need to mourn. And know that you are not alone in this—there are people who understand, who have felt this same pain, and who are walking this path with you.

You and your pet shared a bond that was uniquely yours. **No one else has to understand it for it to matter.**

Why Guilt Is the Hardest Emotion to Process

Grief is painful, but guilt is often what lingers the longest. It's the voice in the back of your mind whispering, *Did I do enough?* It's the replaying of every decision, every moment, searching for something you could have done differently. It's the heavy feeling in your chest that makes it hard to move forward because part of you wonders if you failed the one who depended on you most.

If you're feeling this way, I want you to know something: **guilt is not proof that you did something wrong. It is proof of how much you loved.**

The "Did I Do Enough?" Syndrome

Almost everyone who loses a pet wrestles with the same haunting questions:

- *Did I miss a sign?*
- *Should I have noticed something sooner?*
- *Did I take them to the vet quickly enough?*
- *Did they know how much I loved them?*

The mind becomes a courtroom where you are both the judge and the accused, reviewing every choice, every moment, looking for evidence that you should have done more.

But here's the truth: **loving a pet means doing the best you can with the knowledge you have at the time.** You are not all-knowing. You are not a fortune teller. You made choices out of love, not neglect. And looking back now with more information doesn't mean you failed—it just means you cared enough to want everything to have been perfect.

But perfect doesn't exist. Not in life, and not in death.

Your pet didn't need you to be perfect. They just needed you to love them. And you did.

Euthanasia and Guilt: Making Peace with Difficult Decisions

For those who had to make the painful decision to euthanize, guilt can feel even more overwhelming. It's a unique kind of grief—one that carries the burden of choice.

Even when we know euthanasia is the kindest decision, it never feels *good*. It never feels like *enough*. The moment of saying goodbye can feel unbearable, and after, many people wrestle with thoughts like:

- *Did I do it too soon?*

- *What if they had one more good day left?*

- *Did they know why I made this choice?*

But here's something to hold onto: **Euthanasia is not taking a life. It is taking away suffering.**

If you made this choice, you did it out of love. You put their comfort above your own heartbreak, even though it shattered you. That is not something to feel guilty about— that is something to honor.

Your pet trusted you their whole life. They trusted you to feed them, care for them, and keep them safe. And in the end, they trusted you to help them leave this world with dignity. That is an extraordinary act of love.

If you're struggling with guilt over this decision, try shifting your perspective:

- Instead of **"I ended their life,"** try **"I eased their suffering."**

- Instead of **"I should have waited longer,"** try **"I gave them peace before the pain became unbearable."**

- Instead of **"I made the choice for them,"** try **"They didn't have to go through this alone. I was with them until the end."**

Your pet didn't fear death the way humans do. What they feared was pain, loneliness, and suffering. And because of you, they never had to experience that.

How to Reframe Guilt into Gratitude

Guilt keeps us stuck in the *last* moment. Gratitude allows us to remember the *whole* story.

Right now, your mind might be fixated on the end—what you could have done differently, how you wish things had played out. But your pet's life was so much more than its final moments. It was years of love, companionship, and joy.

Instead of focusing on **what-ifs**, try shifting your focus to **what-was**:

- **Think about all the moments of happiness you gave them.** The belly rubs, the treats, the walks, the cozy afternoons.

- **Remember how safe they felt with you.** You were their world, their comfort, their home.

- **Acknowledge that your love gave them the best life possible.** They didn't just *exist*—they *thrived* because of you.

Every time guilt creeps in, counter it with a memory of love.

- If you're thinking, *"I should have done more,"* remind yourself, *"I gave them a life full of love."*

- If you're wondering, *"Did they know how much I loved them?"* remember how they looked at you, how they followed you, how they sought you out for comfort. **They knew.**

In the end, what mattered most to your pet was not *how* they left this world, but *how* they lived in it—with you.

You were their person. And in their eyes, you were always *enough*.

Anticipatory Grief—Grieving Before the Loss

There's a moment, long before goodbye, when you realize your time together is running out. Maybe your pet is moving slower, their once-playful energy fading. Maybe a vet visit confirmed what you already feared. Or maybe it's just a feeling—an unshakable awareness that the days ahead are fewer than the ones behind.

This is *anticipatory grief*—the heartache that begins *before* a loss even happens. It's mourning in advance, grieving in real-time while your beloved companion is still beside you. And it can be just as painful, if not more, than the grief that comes after.

If you are in this space right now, I want you to know that it's okay to feel what you're feeling. It's okay to cry, to worry, to wish for more time. But it's also possible to walk this road with love instead of fear. And by doing so, you can make the most of the time you have left.

Recognizing and Coping with Pre-Loss Grief

Anticipatory grief often feels like a rollercoaster. One moment, you're soaking in every second, grateful for just one more day. The next, you're overwhelmed by sadness, bracing for the inevitable.

You might find yourself:

- **Tearing up at random moments**, just watching them rest.

- **Feeling helpless**, wishing you could stop time.

- **Swinging between denial and hyper-awareness**, either pretending everything is fine or obsessively monitoring their every breath.

- **Experiencing guilt for grieving too soon**, as if you should "stay strong" while they're still here.

These feelings are all normal. *Loving deeply means grieving deeply,* and your heart is simply trying to process what's coming. But instead of letting fear of the future steal today's joy, you can shift your focus to **making the most of the time you still have.**

Preparing Emotionally While Your Pet Is Still With You

As painful as it is, acknowledging your grief now can help ease the transition later. Instead of pushing your emotions down, allow yourself to *feel* them. Talk to someone who understands—whether it's a friend, a support group, or even your pet itself.

At the same time, take small steps to prepare:

- **Make peace with what you can and cannot control.** You can't stop time, but you *can* choose how you spend it.

- **Have honest conversations with your vet.** Understanding what to expect—whether it's a chronic illness or the natural slowing of age—can help you feel less powerless.

- **Start thinking about how you want to honor them.** Some people find comfort in planning ahead, whether it's choosing a special resting place, gathering photos for a memory book, or deciding on a keepsake that will hold their presence.

And most importantly, **give yourself permission to grieve even while they're still here.** It doesn't mean you're giving up—it means you love them too much to pretend this isn't hard.

Finding Ways to Cherish the Time You Have Left

Instead of letting grief overshadow your final moments together, try shifting your focus to *celebration*. This is still your time together, and it matters.

Some ways to make the most of these days include:

- **Create a "bucket list" of favorite things.** Maybe it's one last trip to their favorite park, a special meal, or simply extra snuggles on the couch.

- **Take more photos and videos.** It may feel bittersweet now, but these small moments will become priceless memories later.

- **Be present.** It's easy to get caught up in what's coming, but your pet is still *here*. Let them feel your love in every moment.

- **Say everything you need to say.** Even if they don't understand your words, they *feel* your emotions. Tell them how much they mean to you.

There's a quote that says, *"One day, all your pet will have is you, and all you will have is them. Make that day beautiful."*

That day may be approaching, but right now, you still have the chance to make *this* day beautiful, too.

Final Thoughts

Anticipatory grief is a painful road, but it's also a gift in disguise. It gives you the opportunity to say goodbye with love, to create moments that will become cherished memories, to ensure that when the time comes, your pet will leave this world knowing they were deeply, fiercely loved.

And when that final moment does come, you'll know— without a doubt—that you made their last days as meaningful as the life they shared with you. **And that is love in its purest form.**

The Role of Rituals in Coping

When we lose a pet, the routines we shared with them suddenly disappear. The morning walks, the evening cuddle sessions, the sound of their paws following us from room to room—gone. The loss isn't just emotional; it's woven into the fabric of our daily lives.

That's why **rituals** can be such a powerful part of healing. They create a bridge between loss and remembrance, giving us a way to **honor the love we shared while learning to move forward**.

Why Rituals Help Process Loss

Grief often feels overwhelming because it's intangible. It's a weight we carry inside, something we *feel* but can't always express. **Rituals give us a way to externalize that grief, to acknowledge it in a way that feels meaningful.**

In human loss, we have funerals, memorials, and anniversaries to mark a loved one's passing. But with pets, those customs aren't built into our culture. We have to create them for ourselves.

Rituals allow us to:

- **Acknowledge the depth of our grief instead of suppressing it.**
- **Honor our pet's impact on our life in a way that feels personal and meaningful.**
- **Create a sense of closure, even if we're not ready to say goodbye.**

And the best part? **There is no right or wrong way to do it.** Whatever brings you comfort, whatever helps you feel connected to your pet's memory—that is the right ritual for you.

Creating a Personal Goodbye Ceremony

A goodbye ceremony doesn't have to be elaborate. It doesn't have to follow any formal tradition. It just needs to be **something that allows you to honor the bond you had**.

Here are some ways you might create a meaningful ritual:

- **Light a candle** in their memory and take a moment to sit with your thoughts.

- **Write them a letter**, expressing all the things you never got the chance to say.

- **Hold a small gathering** with close family or friends who loved them, sharing memories and stories.

- **Scatter their ashes** in a place they loved—by the lake where they swam, under their favorite tree, along a hiking trail you walked together.

- **Create a photo album or scrapbook** filled with memories of their life.

- **Wear a keepsake**—a locket with their picture, a bracelet with their name—something small but meaningful.

If a formal ceremony isn't for you, that's okay. Even something as simple as **taking one last walk in their favorite place** or **placing their collar in a special box** can be a form of honoring them.

The act itself is less important than what it represents: **acknowledging their life, their love, and the space they will always hold in your heart.**

The Healing Power of Storytelling

One of the most comforting ways to keep your pet's memory alive is through storytelling. Talking about them, sharing their quirks, reliving your favorite moments—**these stories are what keep their spirit with you.**

Grief can sometimes make us hesitant to talk about our pets. Maybe we fear it will bring back too much pain. Maybe we worry others won't understand. But the truth is, **remembering them is part of the healing process**.

Tell their story. Not just the sad parts, but the joyful ones:

- The time they stole food right off your plate when you weren't looking.

- The way they *knew* when you needed comfort, curling up beside you without a word.

- The time they got into trouble but looked so proud of themselves you couldn't even be mad.

These moments matter. **They are proof of a life well-lived, a love well-shared.**

If you don't feel ready to talk about them yet, write about them instead. Keep a journal, jot down your favorite memories, create a tribute page—whatever feels right. **Grief is not just about loss. It's about carrying their story forward.**

A Story of Healing: Finding a Way Forward Without Jake

When Jake passed, the silence in the house was unbearable. No more eager paws clicking against the hardwood floor, no more joyful barks greeting me at the door. His bed sat untouched in the corner, his leash still hanging by the door as if I might reach for it out of habit.

For weeks, I felt lost. The mornings were the hardest—waking up and realizing there was no wet nose nudging me awake, no wagging tail waiting for breakfast. I found myself hesitating before stepping inside after work, bracing for the emptiness that followed.

At first, I tried to push the grief away, telling myself to "be strong." But the more I tried to ignore it, the heavier it became. Finally, one afternoon, I sat on the floor beside Jake's bed and let myself cry, really cry. I spoke to him as if he were still there, whispering everything I hadn't said in those final moments.

That night, I lit a candle for him. It was small, simple, but somehow, it made me feel like I was acknowledging his presence instead of just his absence.

Over time, I found little ways to honor him. I framed my favorite photo of him by my bedside. I started going for walks again—at first, they felt empty without him, but soon, they became moments of quiet reflection. I even joined an online pet loss group, where I found comfort in others who understood this unique kind of grief.

One day, I found myself laughing—not just a small chuckle, but a real, deep laugh—when I remembered the time Jake stole an entire sandwich right off my plate. It was the first moment I realized that my grief didn't have to erase the joy of having had him.

Jake may have been gone, but my love for him wasn't. And little by little, I started to heal—not by letting go, but by finding ways to carry him forward with me.

Building a Support System

Grief is heavy. And while healing is a personal journey, **you don't have to carry this weight alone**.

When grieving a pet, finding the right support can make all the difference. But the reality is, **not everyone will understand.**

Some people will minimize your pain. Some will say things like, *"It was just a pet"* or *"You can always get another one."* And that can make grief feel even lonelier.

That's why it's so important to **seek out people who truly understand.**

Finding the Right People to Talk To

Not everyone will be the right person to support you during this time—and that's okay. **Lean on the people who acknowledge your grief, not those who dismiss it.**

Some of the best sources of support include:

- **Friends or family members who have also lost pets**—they know how deep this pain runs.

- **Pet loss support groups**—both in-person and online, these spaces offer a sense of belonging among people who truly understand.

- **Grief counselors or therapists**—especially those who specialize in pet loss, they can provide guidance when the grief feels too heavy to bear alone.

If you don't have anyone in your immediate circle who understands, **consider online communities**. There are pet loss forums, Facebook groups, and even virtual memorial pages where you can share your feelings and memories without fear of judgment.

Grief is easier to carry when it's shared. Even if it's just one person who listens, having someone to talk to can bring immense comfort.

When Professional Help May Be Needed

For many people, pet loss grief is intense but gradually softens over time. But for others, the pain can feel impossible to navigate alone. **If you find yourself unable to function in daily life, struggling with prolonged depression, or feeling like the grief is too much to bear, seeking professional help is a sign of strength, not weakness.**

A therapist who understands pet loss can help you work through feelings of guilt, sadness, and loneliness in a way that feels manageable. **You don't have to do this alone. There is help, and there is hope.**

Final Thoughts

Taking the first steps toward healing doesn't mean "moving on." It doesn't mean forgetting. It simply means learning to carry your grief in a way that allows you to continue living—with love, with remembrance, and with the deep understanding that your pet's impact will never fade.

Grief is not a sign that you're stuck—it's a sign that you loved deeply. And love like that doesn't just disappear.

So take your time. Be kind to yourself. Find ways to honor their memory. And when the days feel especially heavy, remind yourself: **your pet may be gone, but your love for them will always, always remain.**

CHAPTER 2

Breaking Free from the Pain of Guilt and Regret

"If only I had done more..."

The weight of guilt can be heavier than grief itself.

It whispers in the quiet moments, replaying every decision, every missed sign, every moment you wish you could change. It convinces you that somehow, in some way, you could have saved them, that if you had just done *one thing differently*, your pet might still be here.

This is the cruel part of loss—the way it invites doubt, regret, and self-blame to sit beside our sorrow. And for many, this guilt becomes the heaviest burden to carry.

But here's the truth: **guilt is not proof that you failed— it is proof that you loved.** It's what happens when a heart full of love has nowhere to go. And if you are struggling to forgive yourself, know this: *you are not alone, and you are not to blame.*

In this chapter, we'll explore three of the most common sources of guilt—**euthanasia, sudden loss, and past regrets**—and find a way to begin letting go of the pain that is keeping you stuck.

37

Euthanasia Guilt—The Hardest Decision of All

For many pet parents, the most excruciating form of guilt comes from **making the decision to say goodbye.** Even when we know, logically, that euthanasia is a final act of love, our hearts still question:

- *Did I do it too soon?*
- *Did they know I was trying to help them?*
- *What if they had one more good day left?*

If you are wrestling with these thoughts, I want you to hear this: **You made the choice out of love, not out of neglect. Not out of selfishness. Not because you "gave up."**

Why Euthanasia Feels So Heavy

Unlike natural death, which happens on its own timeline, euthanasia places a heartbreaking responsibility in our hands. We become the ones who decide *when* and *how* our pets leave this world. That weight is unbearable at times, making us question whether we had the right to make such a decision at all.

But here's what's important to remember: **your pet didn't fear death. They only feared suffering.**

They didn't understand what was happening the way we do. They didn't count days or measure time. What they knew—what they *felt*—was your presence, your love, your arms holding them in their final moments.

Releasing the Guilt

If you are struggling with the pain of this decision, try shifting your perspective:

- Instead of **"I ended their life,"** say **"I ended their suffering."**

- Instead of **"I took them too soon,"** say **"I gave them peace before the pain became unbearable."**

- Instead of **"I should have done more,"** say **"I did everything I could to make their last moments full of love."**

You didn't fail them. **You freed them.** And that is an act of love beyond words.

Sudden Loss—When There Was No Time to Say Goodbye

Guilt takes on a different shape when loss happens suddenly. There's no time to prepare, no final moments to hold them close, no warning before everything changes in an instant.

If your pet's passing was unexpected—due to an accident, an illness you didn't see coming, or something beyond your control—you might be struggling with thoughts like:

- *I should have been there.*

- *I should have noticed something was wrong.*

- *If only I had done something differently, they would still be here.*

Sudden loss is uniquely painful because it **robs us of closure**. It leaves us searching for answers, replaying the events over and over, trying to find the moment where things could have turned out differently.

But here's the hardest truth to accept: **not everything is in our control.**

Why We Blame Ourselves

When something tragic happens, our brains search for meaning. We want an explanation, a reason—because if we can find the *why*, we think maybe we can prevent the pain from happening again.

But sometimes, there is no reason. Sometimes, no matter how much we loved them, no matter how careful we were, no matter how much we would have done differently, **life is unpredictable, and loss is part of love.**

Letting Go of the "What-Ifs"

If you are trapped in a cycle of regret, remind yourself:

- **You didn't know what you didn't know.** Hindsight makes things seem clearer, but in the moment, you did the best you could.

- **You gave them a life full of love.** That is what mattered most to them—not how they left, but how they lived.

- **They wouldn't want you to suffer.** If they could tell you one thing now, it wouldn't be blame. It would be, *Thank you for loving me.*

The pain of sudden loss is deep. But over time, the shock will soften, and the memories of their life—not just their passing—will take up more space in your heart.

Making Peace with the Past

No matter how your pet passed, **regret has a way of creeping in.** You might find yourself looking back and thinking:

- *I should have spent more time with them.*
- *I should have been more patient.*
- *I should have appreciated them more while they were here.*

Regret is the mind's way of trying to rewrite the past. It's an attempt to make up for lost time, to undo what can't be undone. But holding onto it won't bring them back—it will only keep you trapped in pain.

Turning Guilt into Gratitude

Instead of focusing on what you *wish* you had done, shift your focus to **what you did do**:

- The belly rubs.
- The bedtime snuggles.
- The long walks.

- The moments when they looked at you like you were their whole world—because you were.

Your pet didn't measure your love in perfect moments. They measured it in **the life you gave them, the comfort you provided, the bond you shared.**

You were enough. You did enough.

And now, the best way to honor them isn't to live in regret— it's to carry their love forward.

Maybe that means sharing their story, helping another pet in need, or simply allowing yourself to remember them with more love than pain.

Because at the end of the day, guilt is just love that hasn't found its way to forgiveness yet.

And when you're ready, that love will transform—not into regret, but into something softer, something that brings warmth instead of sorrow.

Something that lets you move forward while still carrying them with you.

A Story of Guilt and Letting Go: Learning to Forgive Myself

When Luna passed, I couldn't stop replaying the last few days of her life in my mind.

She had been slowing down for weeks, struggling to get up from her bed, eating less, sleeping more. I knew she was getting older, but I kept telling myself we had more time. When the vet suggested we start thinking about "next steps," I brushed it off. *She still had good days. She wagged her tail this morning. She's not ready yet.*

But then, one evening, she looked at me differently. Not with pain, not with fear—just a quiet exhaustion. It was as if she was asking me to see what she already knew. I held her all night, my heart breaking with the realization that I had waited too long to accept what was happening.

The guilt was unbearable. *Did I make her suffer longer than she needed to? Should I have made the decision sooner?* The questions gnawed at me, whispering that I had failed her in her final days.

Even after she was gone, I carried that guilt like a weight around my neck. Every time I thought of her, I didn't see the years of love, the thousands of happy moments— weighing her against my mistakes, all I could see was her last few days.

One afternoon, months later, I found one of her old toys under the couch. A small, tattered plush fox she used to carry everywhere. I held it in my hands and, for the first time, let myself remember *all* of her—not just the ending, but the beginning. The way she used to leap into my arms as a puppy. The way she'd press her head into my lap whenever I was upset. The way she'd nudge her bowl when she wanted extra treats.

She had a **good** life. A full life. A life where she was safe, loved, and cherished every single day.

And suddenly, I realized: *Luna wouldn't want my love for her to turn into guilt.*

She didn't keep a record of my mistakes. She didn't measure my love in perfect decisions. She only knew that I was her person, that I had loved her with everything I had.

And that was enough.

That day, I took her toy and placed it on my nightstand—not as a reminder of my guilt, but as a reminder of *her* and the life we shared. And for the first time since losing her, I smiled.

Not because the pain was gone, but because I had finally let myself remember the love more than the loss.

Final Thoughts

Grief is hard enough without guilt weighing you down. Whatever regret you're holding onto, I want you to hear this:

Your pet never held it against you. So maybe, just maybe, it's time to stop holding it against yourself.

Let love be the thing you carry forward—not guilt. Because love is what they left behind. **And love is what will always remain.**

CHAPTER 3

How to Process Your Emotions in a Healthy Way

"The only way out of grief is through it."
– Helen Macdonald

When faced with pet loss, emotions can feel like an uncontrollable storm—waves of sadness, guilt, anger, and even moments of relief. Many struggle with how to express these feelings in a way that allows them to heal rather than remain stuck in suffering. In this chapter, we'll explore how to process emotions healthily, using science-backed strategies and real-life experiences to guide you.

Understanding the Emotional Landscape of Grief

The Spectrum of Grief: More Than Just Sadness

Grief is often thought of as a wave of sadness, a deep and aching sorrow that fills the empty spaces where love once lived. But the truth is, **grief is not just one emotion— it is many.** It is sadness, yes, but it is also longing, guilt, relief, anger, and even, sometimes, unexpected moments of joy.

If your emotions have been all over the place, if one minute you're sobbing and the next you feel nothing at all, know this: **you are not grieving wrong.** There is no single way to grieve. Every emotion you feel is a reflection of the love you shared, and all of them—no matter how conflicting—are valid.

Sadness, Longing, and Despair—How the Depth of Love Reflects the Depth of Grief

Losing a pet isn't just about missing them. It's about the *longing*—the ache of absence, the instinct to reach for them only to remember they're not there. It's about walking through the door and expecting them to greet you. It's about waking up in the middle of the night, thinking you hear their breathing beside you, only to be met with silence.

This kind of grief can feel endless, like an ocean with no shore in sight. Some days, the longing is so strong that it feels unbearable. Other days, it's quieter—just a dull, constant ache that settles into your chest.

This pain, as much as it hurts, is **not a sign of weakness.** It is proof of love. You grieve deeply because you loved deeply. The emptiness you feel now is a reflection of the space they once filled.

And while this sadness may never fully disappear, over time, it will soften. The sharp edges of loss will round out, making room for memories that bring comfort rather than only pain.

Relief and Guilt—Why It's Normal to Feel Relief After a Pet's Passing

One of the most complicated emotions after pet loss is **relief**—and the guilt that often follows it.

If your pet was sick, suffering, or declining for a long time, you may have felt a deep sense of relief when they finally passed. Relief that they are no longer in pain. Relief that they didn't have to struggle anymore. Relief that you no longer have to watch them fade away, powerless to stop it.

And then, almost instantly, guilt creeps in:

- *Does this mean I didn't love them enough?*
- *Shouldn't I have wanted more time with them, no matter what?*
- *What kind of person feels relief after losing someone they love?*

But here's the truth: **Feeling relief does not mean you wanted them to go. It means you wanted their suffering to end.**

Love is selfless. And often, the hardest part of loving a pet is knowing when to let them go. When you've spent days, weeks, or even months watching them struggle, worrying over every change in their health, carrying the emotional weight of knowing what was coming—it is *human* to feel relief when that suffering ends.

Instead of punishing yourself for this feeling, try reframing it:

- Instead of **"I'm relieved they're gone,"** say **"I'm relieved they are free from pain."**

- Instead of **"I shouldn't feel this way,"** say **"It was an honor to love them until their very last moment."**

They wouldn't want you to suffer in their absence. They would want you to remember them with love, not with guilt.

Unexpected Emotions—Anger, Resentment, Numbness, and Even Moments of Joy

Grief is unpredictable. While sadness is often expected, there are other emotions that may surprise you—and each one serves its own purpose in the healing process.

Anger

You might feel anger at:

- The illness or accident that took them.
- The vet who couldn't save them.
- People who don't understand your pain.
- Even your pet for leaving you so soon.

Anger is a natural reaction to loss. It's the mind's way of pushing back against the helplessness of grief. If you find yourself feeling angry, allow yourself to feel it—without guilt. Write about it. Talk about it. Move through it, rather than stuffing it down.

Resentment

Resentment can surface in unexpected ways, too. You might feel resentment toward:

- Friends who still have their pets.
- People who act like your loss isn't "a big deal."
- Even yourself, for choices you made or didn't make.

It's okay to feel this way. Loss makes us hyper-aware of what's missing, and sometimes, that awareness turns into resentment. The key is recognizing it for what it is—a normal, passing emotion—not something that defines you.

Numbness

Not everyone experiences grief as overwhelming sadness right away. Some people feel *nothing*—a strange sense of detachment, like they're watching their life happen from a distance.

This numbness isn't a lack of love—it's a defense mechanism. Sometimes, the brain protects itself from feeling too much all at once. If you're feeling numb, give yourself time. The emotions will come when you're ready to process them.

Moments of Joy

Perhaps the most surprising—and confusing—emotion that can arise during grief is joy.

One day, you might find yourself smiling—*really smiling*—at a memory. You might hear a story about them and laugh.

You might catch yourself feeling happy about something unrelated and immediately feel guilty.

It is okay to feel joy, even in grief.

Loving your pet brought happiness into your life. Their memory can, too. Feeling joy doesn't mean you've "moved on" or that your grief is over. It simply means that love still exists alongside the loss.

Grief and joy are not opposites—they are part of the same experience. And over time, the moments of joy will grow, gently making space for healing.

Final Thoughts

Grief is not just sadness. It is a complex, shifting landscape of emotions—some expected, some surprising, all valid.

There is no right way to grieve. However you are feeling right now—whether it's overwhelming sorrow, quiet relief, unexpected anger, or even fleeting moments of happiness—**it is all part of the journey.**

The only thing you *must* do is allow yourself to feel it. Because when you do, you are not just grieving—you are honoring the love you shared. And **love, even in grief, is never wrong.**

Grief vs. Depression: Knowing the Difference

Losing a pet is heartbreaking, and grief can feel all-consuming. But for most people, grief—while painful—fluctuates. Some days, the sadness feels unbearable, but other days, a warm memory might bring a smile. Over time, the intensity of grief softens, making space for healing.

Depression, on the other hand, is different. It lingers in a way that grief does not. It doesn't come in waves—it settles, making everything feel heavy, isolating, and unchanging.

It's important to understand the difference between **normal grief** and **prolonged distress** so you can recognize when it may be time to seek extra support.

Grief Fluctuates, Depression Lingers

Grief and depression share many similarities—sadness, exhaustion, loss of interest in daily activities—but there's one key difference:

- **Grief comes in waves.** You may feel deep sorrow one moment and a sense of peace the next. You may cry at the sight of their favorite toy, but later, you find comfort in a memory.

- **Depression is constant.** It doesn't come and go. It feels like a heavy fog that won't lift, making even small tasks feel impossible.

If you're grieving, you might:

☑ Have moments of sadness, but also moments of remembering your pet with love.

☑ Feel pain when triggered by reminders but still experience occasional relief.

☑ Miss your pet deeply but remain connected to others and your daily life.

If you're struggling with depression, you might:

▶ Feel a persistent sense of hopelessness, numbness, or emptiness.

▶ Withdraw from family and friends, feeling isolated even when surrounded by people.

▶ Lose interest in things you once enjoyed—not just pet-related activities, but everything.

▶ Struggle with sleep, appetite changes, or overwhelming fatigue that doesn't improve.

Grief is painful, but it still allows room for light. Depression dims everything.

If you're unsure whether you're experiencing grief or something deeper, ask yourself:

- *Am I still able to feel moments of love and connection, even in my sadness?*

- *Do I have days when I feel slightly better, even if only for a short time?*

- *Do I feel like myself, even in my grief, or does it feel like I've lost my sense of identity?*

If grief comes and goes, even if the pain is still raw, that's normal. If it feels like nothing is getting better—**even months later**—it may be time to seek help.

When Grief Turns Into Complicated Grief

Most grief softens with time, but sometimes, it doesn't. **Complicated grief** occurs when someone feels stuck in their sorrow, unable to move forward in a healthy way.

Signs of complicated grief include:

► **Intense, persistent sadness that doesn't improve over time.** If months have passed and the pain still feels as fresh as day one, it may be more than typical grief.

► **Constant feelings of guilt or self-blame.** If guilt dominates your thoughts—believing you failed your pet, questioning your every decision—it can become unhealthy.

► **Avoiding anything that reminds you of your pet.** While some people need time before looking at photos or revisiting memories, avoiding them completely for months or years may signal unresolved grief.

► **Inability to function in daily life.** If work, relationships, or personal care are suffering significantly, it may indicate that grief has turned into something more serious.

► **Persistent feelings of emptiness, hopelessness, or numbness.** If grief has stopped feeling like sadness and instead feels like a deep emotional void, it may be time to seek help.

Complicated grief isn't a sign of weakness—it's simply a sign that your heart is struggling to heal. **And healing is something you don't have to do alone.**

The Role of Professional Help

There is no shame in reaching out for help. **Grief can be overwhelming, and sometimes, we need guidance to navigate it.**

A **grief counselor or therapist** can help if:

☑ You feel stuck in guilt, unable to forgive yourself.

☑ You can't seem to move forward, even after a long time.

☑ The pain is interfering with your ability to function.

☑ You feel hopeless, numb, or disconnected from life.

Therapy doesn't mean forgetting your pet. It means learning how to carry their love forward in a way that allows *you* to live fully again.

Some resources that may help:

- **Pet loss support groups** (both online and in-person)
- **Counselors specializing in pet loss grief**
- **Journaling or expressive writing therapy**
- **Art or music therapy to process emotions differently**

Healing doesn't mean "moving on." It means learning to love them in a new way—one that honors their life without losing yourself in the pain of their loss.

Final Thoughts

Grief and depression may look similar, but they are not the same. Grief shifts, softens, and allows space for love, even in the pain. Depression lingers, making everything feel hollow and unchanging.

If you're grieving, be patient with yourself. But if your grief has turned into something heavier—something that isn't letting you move forward—it's okay to seek support. You don't have to carry this alone.

Your pet would want you to find peace again. **Not to forget them, but to live in a way that honors the love you shared.**

How Unprocessed Grief Affects Your Mind & Body

Grief doesn't just live in the heart—it lives in the body. When we suppress grief, pushing it aside in an attempt to "stay strong" or "move on," it doesn't disappear. It settles deep within us, often in ways we don't recognize until it starts affecting our physical and emotional health.

If you've been feeling exhausted, disconnected, or just *off* since losing your pet, your body may be carrying the weight of unprocessed grief. Science has shown that **unresolved grief can manifest as physical symptoms, emotional distress, and even long-term health issues.** The more we try to ignore or bury our pain, the more it demands to be felt.

Let's explore how grief affects both the **body and mind**, and why acknowledging it is the first step toward healing.

The Connection Between Suppressed Grief and Physical Symptoms

Grief is a **full-body experience**. It triggers stress hormones, disrupts sleep, and alters brain function. Many people who suppress their grief experience a range of physical symptoms, including:

▶ **Fatigue** – Grieving is emotionally exhausting, and when we don't allow ourselves to process it, that exhaustion lingers. Even simple tasks can feel draining.

▶ **Headaches and muscle tension** – Suppressed emotions create stress, and stress causes the body to tense up. This can lead to migraines, back pain, and chronic tightness in the shoulders or jaw.

▶ **Weakened immune system** – Long-term stress caused by unresolved grief can weaken immune function, making you more susceptible to illness, colds, and infections.

▶ **Digestive issues** – The gut and brain are deeply connected. Grief-related stress can cause nausea, stomach pain, and even appetite changes—either a loss of appetite or emotional eating.

These symptoms aren't "just in your head." **They are real, physical responses to unprocessed pain.** Your body is telling you it needs space to grieve.

How Unresolved Grief Manifests Later

When grief isn't acknowledged, it doesn't go away—it finds other ways to surface. Sometimes, this happens immediately. Other times, it can take months or even years.

Here's how unresolved grief often shows up:

▶ **Anxiety and restlessness** – Suppressing grief can lead to a lingering sense of unease, making you feel on edge, irritable, or unable to relax. You may find yourself **constantly busy** as a way to avoid facing your emotions.

▶ **Emotional numbness** – Some people shut down after a loss, feeling disconnected from themselves and others. You might feel like you're going through the motions of life, but nothing really *feels* the same.

▶ **Avoidance behaviors** – You may start avoiding anything that reminds you of your pet—photos, favorite spots, even conversations about them. While this can provide temporary relief, it ultimately prolongs healing.

▶ **Prolonged sadness and difficulty finding joy** – If grief is left unprocessed, it can linger in the background, making happiness feel fleeting or even undeserved. Some people carry a subconscious belief that **if they stop grieving, they are letting go**—but grief and love can coexist.

When grief isn't processed, it can become a **heavy weight** that stays with us far longer than it needs to.

Why Acknowledging Grief Is the Key to Healing

The human brain is designed to process emotions—including grief. Studies show that **when we acknowledge and express painful emotions, we actually lessen their intensity.** This is because the brain processes grief through a network of emotional regulation, and the more we allow ourselves to feel, the more our brain adapts and integrates the loss.

Here's what happens when we allow ourselves to grieve properly:

☑ **Emotions become less overwhelming.** When you talk about your pet, journal, or allow yourself to cry, the pain gradually becomes more manageable.

☑ **Physical symptoms improve.** Suppressing grief keeps the body in a prolonged stress response, but allowing emotions to surface can lower cortisol levels, improve sleep, and reduce muscle tension.

☑ **Healing happens naturally.** Grief isn't something to "fix" or "get over." It's something to move *through*. When you acknowledge your pain instead of avoiding it, healing happens in its own time.

How to Start Processing Grief:

- **Talk about your pet.** Share their story with a friend or write down memories in a journal.

- **Allow yourself to cry.** Tears aren't a sign of weakness—they are your body's natural way of releasing emotion.

- **Create rituals of remembrance.** Light a candle, visit a favorite place, or keep a small memento that brings comfort.

- **Seek support.** Whether it's through a grief counselor, a support group, or an understanding friend, talking about your feelings is an important part of healing.

Grief doesn't demand that we forget—it asks that we remember **in a way that allows us to keep living.**

HOW TO OVERCOME PET LOSS, GRIEF & BEGIN HEALING

Final Thoughts

Unprocessed grief affects both the mind and body in profound ways. Ignoring it doesn't make it disappear—it just forces it to manifest in different forms. **By acknowledging your grief, you're not prolonging the pain—you're giving yourself permission to heal.**

Losing your pet changed you, but it doesn't mean you have to carry this pain forever. In time, as you allow yourself to process your loss, your grief will become something softer. Something that honors your pet's memory rather than weighs you down.

Because healing isn't about letting go—it's about **finding a way to carry their love forward, in a way that brings you peace.**

Healthy Ways to Express and Release Grief: The Power of Writing and Verbal Expression

"There is no greater agony than bearing an untold story inside you." — Maya Angelou

Grief is heavy, and when we keep it bottled up inside, it becomes even heavier. **Expressing grief—through words, stories, or even just speaking out loud—helps release some of that weight.**

Many people struggle to talk about their loss because they fear that bringing it up will make the pain worse. But in reality, sharing your emotions, whether on paper or aloud,

60

can help you process what you're feeling and make space for healing. **Grief needs an outlet.** Writing, talking, and expressing yourself in private or with others allows you to honor your pet's memory while working through the emotions that feel too big to carry alone.

Here are three ways to use words—written or spoken—to help release and process your grief.

Journaling Through Grief

Writing can be a deeply healing practice, allowing you to express emotions you may not feel comfortable saying out loud. The beauty of journaling is that there are no rules— **just a safe space where your grief is free to exist, without judgment.**

Here are a few ways journaling can help:

📝 Writing Letters to Your Pet

One of the most powerful ways to express grief is by writing a letter to your pet. Tell them everything you need them to know—how much you love them, what you miss about them, and even any regrets you're holding onto. **Writing helps your brain process emotions**, making them feel more manageable over time.

- Start with **"Dear [pet's name],"** and let the words flow.

- Tell them about your favorite memories together.

- Share how much they meant to you and what life feels like without them.

- If you're feeling guilty about something, express it—then try to let it go.

Many people find comfort in **reading the letter out loud**, lighting a candle afterward, or keeping it in a special place to revisit when they need to feel close to their pet.

📝 Gratitude Journaling

Grief often focuses on **what we lost**, but gratitude shifts our perspective to **what we had**. Writing down even small moments of gratitude can help soften the pain and bring warmth to your memories.

Try this prompt: *"Today, I am grateful that my pet taught me _____."*

- Maybe they taught you patience, unconditional love, or how to be present.
- Maybe they helped you through a difficult time in your life.
- Maybe they made you laugh in ways no one else could.

Focusing on gratitude doesn't mean ignoring your grief—it simply helps remind you that **their love was a gift that will always be part of you.**

📝 Daily Reflections

Some people find comfort in simply **writing about their feelings each day**, without any structure. Letting your thoughts spill onto the page—whether you're feeling sad, angry, relieved, or numb—helps release emotions rather than letting them build up inside.

Even just five minutes of writing a day can help you process your grief in a healthy way.

Talking About Your Pet: Why Sharing Memories Helps Keep Their Love Alive

Grief often makes us want to withdraw. We worry that bringing up our pet will make others uncomfortable. Maybe we fear that talking about them will make the pain worse.

But the opposite is true. **Talking about your pet keeps their love alive.**

Think about it: When we lose a human loved one, we tell stories about them. We reminisce about their laugh, their quirks, the way they made us feel. **The same should be true for our pets.**

Ways to keep your pet's memory alive through conversation:

🐾 **Say Their Name:** It might hurt at first, but keeping their name in your life helps you feel connected to them. Instead of saying, *"My dog used to do that,"* try, *"Max used to do that."* Their name is part of their story, and it deserves to be spoken.

🐾 **Share Favorite Memories:** Tell the funny, heartwarming, or even mischievous stories that made your pet unique. Share with family, friends, or even in a pet loss support group. Talking about them out loud helps shift your focus from just their loss to the beautiful life they lived.

🐾 **Create a Tradition:** Maybe it's setting aside one day a month to talk about them with a loved one. Maybe it's bringing up a favorite memory whenever you see another pet that reminds you of them. Talking about them regularly helps integrate their memory into your life rather than pushing it away.

🐾 **Let Yourself Laugh:** At first, it might feel impossible. But one day, you'll remember something silly they did—the way they got zoomies after a bath, or how they always managed to steal your spot on the couch—and you'll smile. And when that happens, **let it happen.** Laughter and joy don't erase grief. They are part of healing.

Recording Voice Notes: Speaking Your Thoughts Aloud to Process Emotions Privately

Not everyone is comfortable journaling, and not everyone has someone to talk to about their grief. But **speaking your emotions aloud—even just to yourself—can be incredibly therapeutic.**

🎙 **Why Voice Notes Help:** Recording your thoughts **helps externalize grief**, similar to journaling. Saying what you're feeling out loud allows you to release emotions in a safe, private way. It's like talking to a trusted friend—except that friend is you.

If you're unsure where to start, try:

- **Recording a message to your pet.** Talk to them as if they're still there.

- **Speaking through your emotions in the moment.** Say, *"Right now, I feel..."* and just let it flow.

- **Talking about a favorite memory.** Describe it in detail, reliving the happiness.

Some people find comfort in **saving** these recordings, while others choose to delete them after speaking. There's no right way—just whatever feels healing for you.

Final Thoughts

Grief needs expression. Holding it in only makes it heavier. Whether through **writing, talking, or recording your thoughts**, finding a way to **release your emotions** will help you process the pain in a way that leads to healing.

Your pet's love deserves to be remembered—not just in silence, but in **stories, in laughter, in the words you choose to carry forward.**

Because as long as you speak their name, **they are never truly gone.**

Mindfulness and Emotional Regulation Techniques

Grief has a way of pulling us out of the present moment. One minute, you're going about your day, and the next, a wave of sorrow crashes over you—sometimes triggered by a memory, sometimes by nothing at all. It can feel like you're drowning in emotions with no way to regain control.

This is where **mindfulness and emotional regulation techniques** can help. These practices don't take away grief (and they're not meant to), but they **help you navigate it** in a way that allows you to feel your emotions without being consumed by them.

By using mindfulness techniques like **grounding, breathwork, and emotional acceptance**, you can gently guide yourself back to the present moment—helping you process your grief instead of feeling stuck in it.

Grounding Exercises: Using the Five Senses to Stay Present

When grief feels overwhelming, grounding techniques can help bring you back to the present. These exercises use **your five senses** to reconnect you with the world around you, creating a sense of stability during moments of emotional distress.

5-4-3-2-1 Grounding Exercise

This simple but powerful technique helps calm racing thoughts by focusing on what's happening *right now*.

🌿 **Five things you can see** – Look around and name five objects near you (a tree, a book, a piece of furniture, the sky, your hands).

🌿 **Four things you can touch** – Notice the textures around you (your clothing, a pet's fur, a soft blanket, the ground beneath your feet).

🌿 **Three things you can hear** – Tune into sounds you may not usually notice (birds outside, a ticking clock, your own breathing).

🌿 **Two things you can smell** – Inhale deeply and identify scents (coffee, fresh air, lotion, the scent of your pet's belongings).

🌿 **One thing you can taste** – If possible, take a sip of water, tea, or a small piece of food to bring your focus back to the present.

This exercise helps **anchor you in reality** when grief feels overwhelming. The goal isn't to push away your emotions but to create a sense of balance—allowing you to feel your grief *without losing yourself in it.*

Breathwork and Meditation: Techniques to Calm Overwhelming Emotions

Grief affects the nervous system, often putting the body into **a state of stress and tension**. This is why you might experience shallow breathing, a tight chest, or a racing heartbeat when emotions become too much to bear.

Breathwork and meditation are simple but effective ways to **calm your nervous system** and bring a sense of peace, even in the midst of grief.

Box Breathing (4-4-4-4 Technique)

This structured breathing exercise helps regulate emotions by slowing the heart rate and reducing stress.

☐ **Inhale deeply for 4 seconds.**

☐ **Hold your breath for 4 seconds.**

☐ **Exhale slowly for 4 seconds.**

☐ **Pause for 4 seconds before inhaling again.**

Repeat this cycle several times. As you breathe, imagine **inhaling calm and exhaling grief**—letting go, little by little.

Guided Meditation for Grief

If your mind feels too restless for traditional meditation, try a **guided grief meditation**. These are audio or video recordings where a calming voice leads you through a process of **relaxation, emotional acceptance, and remembrance.**

- YouTube, meditation apps, and pet loss support groups often offer free guided sessions.

- Focus on ones that encourage **gentle self-compassion** rather than forcing "letting go."

- Even just **5–10 minutes a day** can help ease emotional distress.

Meditation isn't about *erasing* grief—it's about **creating moments of stillness** where you can breathe through it.

Emotional Acceptance vs. Suppression: Sitting with Grief Without Being Consumed by It

Many people believe that if they fully **allow** themselves to feel grief, they will break down completely—unable to function or move forward. As a result, they suppress their emotions, **pushing pain aside rather than confronting it.**

But here's the truth: **Avoiding grief doesn't make it go away. It makes it stay longer.**

What Emotional Suppression Looks Like

🚫 Keeping yourself *too busy* to think about your loss.

🚫 Avoiding reminders of your pet (photos, their belongings, talking about them).

🚫 Feeling numb or disconnected, as if you're on autopilot.

🚫 Telling yourself you "should be over it by now."

What Emotional Acceptance Looks Like

☑ Allowing yourself to feel without judgment.

☑ Acknowledging grief as a natural part of love, rather than something to "fix."

✅ Giving yourself space to cry, talk, or express emotions without guilt.

✅ Understanding that grief is not linear—it comes in waves, and that's okay.

How to Sit With Grief Without Letting It Consume You

- **Schedule time for grief.** If you feel overwhelmed, give yourself 10–15 minutes a day to fully feel your emotions—whether it's through journaling, crying, or simply sitting in reflection. When time is up, shift to something comforting (a walk, a book, a warm bath).

- **Acknowledge pain without self-judgment.** If grief suddenly hits you, instead of pushing it away, try saying: *"This is grief, and it's okay. I miss them because I loved them."*

- **Use grounding techniques to stay balanced.** When emotions become too intense, return to breathwork, meditation, or sensory grounding exercises.

Sitting with grief doesn't mean **staying stuck in sadness forever.** It means **making space for healing by allowing emotions to flow naturally.**

A Story of Breath and Healing: Learning to Breathe Again After Losing Bella

When Bella passed, I felt like I couldn't breathe.

She had been my shadow for eleven years, always by my side, always there to remind me that no matter how hard life got, I was never truly alone. But the day she was gone, the air in the house felt heavier, like a weight pressing down on my chest. Every time I thought about her—her wagging tail, her gentle eyes—I felt my throat tighten, my heart race. Grief wasn't just emotional; it was physical.

One night, a few days after she passed, I found myself sitting in my car, gripping the steering wheel, struggling to catch my breath. It had been a long, exhausting day of holding everything in, pretending I was okay when I wasn't. And suddenly, it hit me all at once—the sadness, the emptiness, the unbearable silence of a world without Bella.

I felt like I was drowning in it.

That's when I remembered something a friend had told me: *When grief feels too heavy, focus on your breath. One inhale, one exhale. That's all you have to do.*

So, I closed my eyes, placed my hand over my heart, and started a simple pattern:

☐ Inhale for four seconds.

☐ Hold for four seconds.

☐ Exhale for four seconds.

At first, it felt impossible. My mind kept screaming, *She's gone, she's gone, she's gone.* But I kept breathing.

Inhale. Hold. Exhale.

With each breath, the panic loosened just a little. My shoulders relaxed. My heartbeat slowed. The pain was still there, but I was no longer drowning in it.

For the first time since Bella left, I felt something other than overwhelming sadness. I felt grounded. Present. Just *here*, in this moment, with my breath.

That night, I didn't fix my grief. I didn't stop missing her. But I learned something important—grief takes your breath away, but you can take it back. One inhale at a time.

Final Thoughts

Mindfulness, grounding exercises, and emotional acceptance don't take grief away—but they **help you move through it with more peace and less overwhelm.**

By giving yourself **the space to feel, the tools to calm your nervous system, and the permission to grieve without judgment**, you create a path toward healing that honors both your pain and the love that remains.

Because grief is not the absence of love—it is **love, transformed.**

The Role of Art, Music, and Movement in Healing

Grief lives in the body. It settles in the heart, the mind, and the muscles. It lingers in the quiet moments, in the memories that come rushing back when we least expect them. But just as grief takes up space within us, **we can find ways to release it**—through creativity, music, and movement.

When words feel too heavy, **art, music, and physical movement** offer alternative paths for healing. Whether through painting, listening to songs that remind you of your pet, or simply going for a walk, these forms of expression help process grief in ways that feel natural and deeply personal.

Creative Expression as Therapy

Sometimes, grief feels too big for words. That's where **art** can help. Creativity gives us a way to **externalize our emotions**, to take what's inside and put it into something tangible.

🎨 **Painting or Drawing** – Expressing grief visually can be incredibly therapeutic. Some people paint portraits of their pets, while others create abstract pieces that reflect their emotions. There is no right or wrong—only a chance to create **without judgment.**

📖 **Scrapbooking or Journaling** – Gathering photos, writing memories, and crafting a scrapbook dedicated to your pet can help keep their story alive. Looking through old pictures can be painful at first, but over time, it becomes a way to celebrate the love you shared.

🐾 **Creating a Memorial Piece** – Whether it's a shadow box filled with their collar and favorite toy, a handmade bracelet with their name, or a digital collage of favorite moments, **making something in their honor** allows you to channel grief into something meaningful.

Art isn't about skill—it's about **giving grief a place to go**.

Music and Its Connection to Emotion

Music has a way of reaching places words cannot. A single song can bring back a flood of memories, remind us of a specific moment, or simply make us feel understood in our grief.

🎵 **Creating a Playlist for Your Pet:** One powerful way to honor your pet is to put together a playlist of songs that remind you of them. These could be:

- Songs that were playing during special moments.
- Lyrics that resonate with your emotions.
- Instrumental music that brings a sense of peace.

Some people find comfort in listening to **soothing, meditative music**, while others need **melancholic songs that let them fully feel their grief**. Whatever speaks to you in the moment, let music be part of your healing journey.

🎧 Using Music for Emotional Release

- If you need to **cry**, play the songs that open your heart.

- If you need to **calm your mind**, try instrumental or nature sounds.

- If you need **a reminder of joy**, listen to upbeat songs that remind you of happy times with your pet.

Music **meets you where you are**—whether you need comfort, expression, or just a way to sit with your emotions.

Physical Movement to Release Emotional Energy

Grief isn't just emotional—it's **physical**. It creates tension in the body, making the chest feel heavy, the shoulders tight, the stomach uneasy. Movement helps **release some of that tension**, allowing grief to flow through rather than stay stuck inside.

🧍 **Walking** – Simply taking a walk, especially in nature, can help **clear the mind and process emotions**. If your pet loved a particular walking route, revisiting it can be a way to honor them. Some people even find comfort in talking to their pet while they walk, imagining them still by their side.

🧘 **Yoga & Stretching** – Gentle movement can help ease **grief-related stress** in the body. Certain yoga poses, like child's pose or heart-opening stretches, encourage **deep breathing and relaxation**, helping release sadness stored in the muscles.

💃 **Dance & Free Movement** – Sometimes, grief carries **restless energy** that needs an outlet. Playing music and allowing yourself to **move freely, without structure or expectation**, can help process deep emotions. Whether

75

it's slow swaying or expressive movement, **let your body lead the way.**

Grief **isn't just something we feel—it's something we hold.** And by moving, we give ourselves permission to release it.

Final Thoughts

Healing doesn't just happen in stillness—it happens in **creation, in sound, in movement.** Whether through painting, listening to music, or simply walking outside, these small acts help grief **shift** rather than stay stuck.

There is no right way to grieve. But through art, music, and movement, you can **find your own way forward—one step, one song, one brushstroke at a time.**

Transforming Pain into Meaningful Action: Honoring Your Pet Through Purpose

Grief is love that has nowhere to go. When we lose a pet, that love doesn't disappear—it lingers, seeking a way to express itself. One of the most powerful ways to navigate grief is by **turning pain into purpose**—by honoring your pet in a way that gives their memory lasting meaning.

By **giving back, advocating for animals, or performing acts of kindness in their name**, you can channel your sorrow into something that brings comfort—not just to yourself, but to others who may need it.

Turning Grief into Advocacy

Many people who have experienced deep loss find healing in **helping other animals in need**. If your pet filled your life with love, continuing their legacy by **supporting animal welfare causes** can be a meaningful way to honor them.

🐾 **Volunteer at a Local Animal Shelter** – Spending time with animals in need—whether by walking dogs, fostering kittens, or helping with adoption events—allows you to **give love to those who need it most**.

🐾 **Donate in Your Pet's Name** – Contributing to an animal rescue, sponsoring a pet's medical care, or even donating supplies (food, blankets, toys) to a shelter **keeps your pet's spirit alive through generosity.**

🐾 **Advocate for Animal Welfare** – Some people find purpose in **raising awareness about pet adoption, proper pet care, or supporting spay/neuter programs**. Using your experience to help others become better pet guardians can be an empowering way to turn loss into impact.

🐾 **Start a Pet Loss Support Group** – If you've struggled with the loneliness of grief, you're not alone. **Creating a space—whether online or in person— where people can share memories, emotions, and healing strategies** can be a profound way to give back.

Grief can feel isolating, but **advocacy connects us with something larger than ourselves.** It reminds us that while our pet may be gone, **our love for them can still create positive change.**

Memorializing Through Meaningful Actions

Sometimes, the best way to honor your pet's life is through **acts of kindness that reflect the love they brought into the world.**

💜 **Perform Acts of Kindness in Their Name:** Doing something kind for another person or animal—whether small or big—can help transform grief into something beautiful.

- **Pay for a pet's adoption fee** at a shelter.

- **Bake homemade treats for a friend's pet** in memory of your own.

- **Leave kindness notes** in your neighborhood dog park: *"In memory of a special soul, hug your pet a little tighter today."*

- **Sponsor a therapy animal** to bring comfort to others in need.

🌿 **Plant a Memorial Garden or Tree:** Many people find healing in **planting something that grows in honor of their pet**—a flowerbed, a tree, or even a small indoor plant. Watching it flourish can serve as a reminder that **love continues, even after loss.**

🕯️ **Create a Ritual of Remembrance:** A simple but meaningful way to keep your pet's memory alive is to **set aside time each year (or even each month) to honor them.**

- Light a candle in their honor.

- Visit a place they loved.

- Write them a letter or share a memory with someone who knew them.

Memorializing isn't about dwelling in the past—it's about **keeping their presence alive in a way that brings warmth instead of only sorrow.**

How Giving Back Can Accelerate Healing

There's a reason why **acts of service** have been shown to reduce grief and improve emotional well-being. Studies in psychology show that **when we shift focus from our own pain to helping others, it creates a sense of purpose and connection**—two things that can feel lost in the depths of grief.

☑ **Giving back creates meaning.** Instead of focusing on what was lost, it allows you to build something that continues your pet's impact.

☑ **Helping others fosters connection.** Whether with animals or fellow pet lovers, acts of kindness remind us that we are not alone.

☑ **Taking action empowers healing.** Grief can feel helpless, but making a difference—big or small—gives you a sense of control over how you carry your pet's memory forward.

Your pet brought love, comfort, and companionship into your life. **By finding ways to reflect that love into the world, you ensure that their presence remains— not just in your heart, but in the hearts of those you touch.**

A Story of Remembrance: Lily's Bench

When Sarah lost Lily, her golden retriever of 14 years, the world felt unbearably quiet. The house, once filled with the soft sound of Lily's paws padding across the floor, now echoed with silence. The morning walks they had taken together for years suddenly felt pointless.

For weeks, Sarah found herself stuck in the depths of grief, unable to move forward. She wanted to do something—*anything*—to honor Lily, but nothing seemed big enough to capture the love they had shared.

One morning, she found herself walking the familiar trail at the park where she and Lily had spent countless mornings together. She stopped at their usual resting spot—a quiet clearing by the lake, where Lily would sit patiently beside her, watching the water ripple.

That's when she knew.

She reached out to the local park service and arranged to have a **memorial bench** placed in that very spot. A simple wooden bench, with a small plaque that read:

"In loving memory of Lily—forever my best friend and adventure buddy."

The day the bench was installed, Sarah sat there for the first time without Lily by her side. The grief was still there, but so was something else—**a sense of peace**. Now, whenever she visited, she wasn't just mourning Lily's absence—she was **celebrating the life they had shared**.

Over time, she noticed others stopping at the bench—dog walkers, families, people needing a quiet moment. Some sat in silence, some read the plaque, some even brought their own dogs to rest there for a while. It comforted her to know that Lily's presence lived on in that spot, offering peace to others just as she had to Sarah.

And on the hardest days, when the loss felt overwhelming, Sarah would return to the bench, close her eyes, and imagine Lily sitting beside her once again—watching the water, just like they always had.

Final Thoughts

Grief is love transformed. It doesn't have to end with loss— it can become **something meaningful, something lasting, something that honors the bond you shared.**

Whether through **advocacy, acts of kindness, memorials, or simply sharing their story**, your pet's memory doesn't have to fade.

Because love like that doesn't just disappear. **It continues—through you.**

Creating a Grief Ritual to Support Healing

Grief is not something to "get over"—it's something to move through. And while time does help soften the sharp edges of loss, **intentional rituals** can provide structure, comfort, and a sense of connection to your pet long after they're gone.

Rituals give us a way to honor our emotions, process our pain, and ensure that our pet's memory remains a part of our lives. Whether it's lighting a candle, visiting a favorite place, or setting aside a specific day to remember them, **small, repeated actions** help grief feel less overwhelming and more like a continued bond.

Setting a Grief Timeline

One of the most important things to remember about grief is that **it has no set expiration date.** However, giving yourself a **loose timeline** can help create a sense of movement—allowing space for mourning while also ensuring that grief does not consume your life indefinitely.

✅ Give yourself permission to mourn.

Grief is valid, and it doesn't need to be rushed. If you need weeks, months, or even longer to process your loss, that's okay. **Allow yourself to feel, without guilt.**

✅ Set healthy boundaries.

While grief is natural, **it shouldn't take away your ability to function** in daily life. If you find that sadness is preventing you from engaging with loved ones, working, or taking care of yourself, consider setting small but achievable goals for re-engagement.

☑ Allow for transition points.

A grief timeline doesn't mean saying goodbye—it means creating a gentle transition toward healing. For example:

- *"For the first month, I will give myself time to grieve without pressure. After that, I will begin small steps toward reintroducing joy."*

- *"I will set a date in the future to create a permanent memorial for my pet, so I know I have something to look forward to."*

Grief timelines aren't about **ending grief**—they're about **giving it space to evolve naturally** while making room for healing.

Designing Personal Rituals

Rituals can provide comfort, structure, and a **meaningful way to stay connected to your pet**. They don't have to be elaborate—just something that **feels right for you**.

🐾 **Lighting a Candle** – Set aside a time to light a candle for your pet, whether on special dates or whenever you need a moment of remembrance. The simple act of lighting a flame can symbolize their presence continuing to shine in your life.

🐾 **Visiting a Special Place** – If your pet had a favorite park, beach, or backyard spot, visiting that place can help **keep their spirit alive in a space they loved**. Even sitting there quietly, remembering them, can bring comfort.

🐾 **Creating a "Grief Anniversary"** – Marking a day each year (or even each month) to reflect on your pet's life **can turn sorrow into a celebration of love**. Some people:

- Make a special meal they used to share with their pet.
- Donate to an animal shelter in their pet's name.
- Spend time looking through old pictures and videos.

🐾 **Writing a Letter** – Some people find healing in writing to their pet on special days. Whether it's a simple **"I still miss you"** or a longer letter about how life has changed, **writing can be a way to maintain connection**.

🐾 **Creating a Memorial Ritual** – Whether it's planting a tree, keeping their tag on a necklace, or setting up a small remembrance altar, having **a dedicated space for grief and love** can be healing.

There's no right or wrong ritual—**only what feels comforting to you**.

A Story of Ritual and Healing: Milo's Morning Walk

When James lost Milo, his loyal Labrador of ten years, the mornings became unbearable. For a decade, his day had started the same way—Milo waking him up with a wet nose against his hand, stretching as he waited by the door for their morning walk. Rain or shine, those walks were their ritual, a quiet time just for the two of them.

But now, there was only silence.

For weeks, James avoided their usual route. He couldn't bear to walk the familiar path alone. Every time he saw another dog with their owner, his chest tightened with grief. It felt like walking without Milo would be a betrayal, like moving forward meant leaving him behind.

Then, one morning, James found Milo's old leash still hanging by the door. Instead of breaking down, he took it in his hands and whispered, *Let's go for a walk, buddy.*

With the leash tucked in his pocket, he stepped outside and started down their old path—not as a way to move on, but as a way to **keep moving with Milo in his heart**.

Each day, he made it part of his morning ritual:

🐾 Walking the same trail they used to take together.

🐾 Stopping at Milo's favorite bench, sitting for a few minutes in quiet remembrance.

🐾 Saying, *"Good morning, Milo,"* before heading home.

Over time, the pain softened. The first few walks were heavy with sadness, but as the days passed, they became a **time for reflection, for gratitude, for connection.** He started noticing little signs—paw prints in the dirt, the way the sun filtered through the trees just right, a dog that looked at him the way Milo used to.

One morning, he met another dog owner who had recently lost her pup. She told him she had been struggling to go on walks too, and James shared his ritual with her. Soon, she started doing the same—walking not just for her pet, but with them, in spirit.

Milo's walks became more than just a routine—they became a bridge between **grief and healing, past and present, loss and love.**

And though Milo was no longer by his side, James never truly walked alone.

The Importance of Consistency

Small, repeated actions over time can **help grief feel less chaotic and more manageable**. Rituals create **a sense of rhythm**, ensuring that loss doesn't feel like an abrupt ending but rather **a continued relationship, redefined in a new way**.

🔳 **Why consistency helps healing:**

✔ **Rituals provide stability** when emotions feel overwhelming.

✔ **They create intentional moments** for processing grief rather than letting it control you.

✔ **Over time, they shift grief into gratitude**, helping you remember love instead of just loss.

Healing doesn't happen all at once—it happens **in small, intentional ways, over time**.

By creating personal rituals that feel meaningful to you, you **honor your grief, honor your pet, and create space for both healing and remembrance.**

Because grief is not about forgetting—it's about **carrying love forward in a way that brings you peace.**

Finding a New Emotional Anchor

Losing a pet can feel like losing part of yourself. They were not just a companion—they were part of your daily life, your source of comfort, your steady presence in a chaotic world. When they're gone, it's easy to feel untethered, as if grief has left you drifting without direction.

But healing begins when you find **a new emotional anchor**—not to replace your pet, but to create **new sources of connection, gratitude, and love** that help you move forward while still carrying their memory.

Replacing Loss with Connection

One of the most painful parts of pet loss is the sudden absence of companionship. The quiet spaces where they used to be, the routines that now feel empty—**grief thrives in isolation**. That's why finding new ways to **connect** is essential for healing.

🐾 Seek companionship in community.

Grief can be lonely, but you don't have to go through it alone. Talking to others who have experienced pet loss— whether in a support group, an online forum, or with close friends—can remind you that your emotions are valid and that healing is possible.

🌿 Find solace in nature.

Many people find comfort in spending time outside—walking in a park, sitting in the sun, or even gardening. Nature has a way of grounding us, reminding us that life continues in gentle, healing ways.

🔄 Create new routines that honor the love you shared.

If you're struggling with a lost daily habit—like morning walks, playtime, or mealtime—try repurposing it into something meaningful.

- If you always took your pet for a morning walk, continue the habit and **use the time for reflection and remembrance.**

- If feeding time was a special moment, consider **volunteering at an animal shelter** to help care for other pets in need.

- If you miss their presence during quiet moments, **create a small memorial space in your home** where you can sit and feel close to them.

Connection doesn't mean forgetting—it means **rebuilding life in a way that keeps their love present in new, fulfilling ways.**

The Power of Gratitude in Healing

Grief focuses on what was lost, but gratitude reminds us of what was *given*. While the pain of losing your pet is real, so is the **joy, love, and warmth they brought into your life.** Shifting your focus to **appreciation rather than absence** can help transform grief into something more gentle, more bearable.

Ways to practice gratitude while grieving:

💜 **Write down what you're thankful for.**

Take a moment each day to reflect on the happy times you shared. Instead of thinking *"I lost them too soon,"* try *"I was lucky to have them at all."*

🐾 **Celebrate the small moments.**

Your pet's love still exists in **memories, in lessons, in the way they shaped you**. Maybe they taught you patience, loyalty, or how to live in the present. Hold onto those lessons.

✨ **Turn grief into appreciation.**

Instead of feeling the ache of their absence, try saying *"Thank you"* for every moment you had with them. *Thank you for the snuggles, the adventures, the unconditional love.* Gratitude doesn't erase grief, but it **helps soften its sharpest edges.**

Carrying Love Forward

Healing doesn't mean leaving your pet behind—it means **finding a way to carry their love forward in a way that brings you peace instead of pain.**

🐶 **Integrate their memory into your daily life.**

- Keep a small reminder of them—a framed photo, their collar, or a keepsake that brings comfort.
- Say their name out loud when you think of them. **They are still part of your story.**

🐾 **Honor them through kindness.**

- Help another pet in need, whether by volunteering, donating, or fostering.

- Perform acts of kindness in their name, such as leaving pet treats at a shelter or sponsoring an adoption fee.

💬 **Keep talking about them.**

- Share their story with others.

- Laugh at the silly things they used to do.

- Keep their presence alive through memories, not just sorrow.

Your pet's love doesn't have to be confined to the past. It can continue **shaping your life, your choices, and the way you love going forward.**

Final Thoughts

Finding a new emotional anchor doesn't mean replacing the love you lost—it means **finding new ways to carry it with you.** By seeking connection, practicing gratitude, and carrying their love forward, you allow healing to happen in a way that honors **both your grief and the deep, beautiful bond you shared.**

Because love like that doesn't end—it simply finds new ways to live on.

Final Takeaway for This Chapter

Grief is complex, deeply personal, and never follows a straight path. But **allowing yourself to process it in a**

healthy way is what ultimately leads to healing.
There is no single "right" way to grieve—only the way that
feels **authentic to you**.

What matters most is that you **express your emotions
rather than suppress them.** Whether through writing,
talking, movement, or creating a meaningful ritual, giving
your grief a voice allows it to soften over time.

Your love for your pet was real, and so is your grief. But
healing doesn't mean forgetting—it means learning to
carry their memory with more love than pain.

Action Step:

Choose **one** emotional processing technique from this
chapter—whether it's journaling, talking about your pet,
breathwork, or creating a ritual—and **commit to
practicing it for the next seven days.** See how it feels
to honor your emotions rather than push them away.

Because healing happens in small, intentional steps—and
every step forward is one taken with love.

Hello,

I hope you are finding this book useful as you work your way along the difficult path toward healing. I continue to use many of the techniques and guidance in this book including, for example, some memory routines.

I know for me, personally, it was tough writing this book as it brought back many memories mostly happy but some sad.

Before you begin the next chapter, it would really mean a lot to me if you spent a few minutes and left a book review.

I am a self-published author and one of the best ways for me to get feedback is from you so that I can continue to write and publish books that help improve our lives.

Amazon US:

"Healing doesn't mean forgetting; it means learning to smile at the memories instead of crying at the loss."

Thank you once again and I hope you enjoy the rest of the book.

With warmest wishes and sending love your way,

Andre St Pierre

CHAPTER 4

Coping with the Daily Void— Handling Triggers and Empty Spaces

"It's not just the big moments that hurt the most— it's the small ones. The empty food bowl, the absence of tiny footsteps, the quiet where there was once life."

One of the hardest aspects of losing a beloved pet is dealing with the daily routines and quiet spaces they leave behind. Grief is not just about the loss itself—it's about learning how to navigate life without them. This chapter will provide practical strategies to handle emotional triggers, adjust to new routines, and find ways to fill the void without feeling like you're "moving on" too soon.

Understanding Why the Absence Feels So Overwhelming: The Role of Routine in Pet Bonding

Grief isn't just about missing your pet—it's about **missing the rhythm of life they created with you.**

93

Pets don't just exist in our lives; they shape our **daily routines, our habits, and even our subconscious expectations**. From the way they greeted us in the morning to the quiet moments before bed, they were woven into the fabric of our day in ways we often didn't fully realize—until they were gone.

This is why their absence feels so overwhelming. **It's not just emotional—it's mental, physical, and deeply ingrained in the way we lived.**

How Pets Shape Our Daily Habits

Every pet owner builds routines—some intentional, some automatic. These routines **structure our days and give us a sense of connection and purpose.**

🐾 **Morning Greetings** – Whether it was waking up to their excited tail wags, soft meows, or the weight of their body curled beside you, mornings began **with their presence.**

🐾 **Mealtime Rituals** – Feeding them wasn't just a chore—it was an interaction, a moment of care and bonding that happened like clockwork.

🐾 **Walks, Playtime, and Training** – The structured moments of movement and engagement kept both you and your pet on a **predictable schedule.**

🐾 **Evening Wind-Downs** – Maybe they followed you to bed, curled up on the couch, or simply **rested nearby** as you ended your day.

When these routines suddenly disappear, it can feel like life has lost its natural rhythm. It's not just the **loss of a pet—** it's the loss of **everything they brought to each part of the day.**

The Subconscious Expectations of Their Presence

Our brains are wired for pattern recognition. When we repeat behaviors and experiences, our minds build **expectations** around them—so much so that they become automatic.

💬 **You might still instinctively...**

- **Look for them when you wake up**—expecting them to be in their usual spot.

- **Listen for their footsteps** when coming home, even though you know they're gone.

- **Reach for their leash, bowl, or favorite toy** before realizing they're no longer there.

These moments can be **jarring** because they remind us that grief isn't just emotional—it's deeply **neurological.** The brain continues to search for familiar patterns, struggling to adjust to the absence of something that was once a fundamental part of daily life.

And when the reality sets in? **It feels disorienting, like a world suddenly out of sync.**

Why Loss Feels Disorienting: The Impact of Disrupted Routines on Mental Well-Being

Routines create a sense of **stability and emotional grounding.** When we lose a pet, those routines are abruptly disrupted, making the world feel **unfamiliar and even chaotic.**

🖤 **The brain craves structure.** Without the daily cues that a pet provides, life can feel scattered, as if something essential is missing—but you can't quite put it into words.

🖤 **Grief is exhausting.** The mental effort required to *relearn* how to go through the day without your pet takes an emotional toll. Even simple things, like waking up or eating meals, may feel **off-balance** for a while.

🖤 **Loneliness is amplified.** If your pet was a primary source of companionship, their absence leaves behind **not just emptiness, but silence.** This can trigger deeper feelings of isolation, even when surrounded by people.

It's important to recognize that **feeling lost after a pet's passing is normal**—not just because of grief, but because your brain and body are trying to adjust to a **new way of being**.

Final Thoughts

The overwhelming absence you feel isn't just about missing your pet—it's about missing the **daily moments of connection, comfort, and routine** they provided. Their presence shaped your life in ways you may not have realized, and now, your brain is struggling to make sense of the sudden change.

Be patient with yourself. **Adjusting takes time.** And while the routines you once shared with your pet may no longer exist in the same way, you can gently build **new routines that honor their memory** while helping you move forward.

Because love doesn't disappear with loss—it simply finds new ways to exist. 🖤

Why Triggers Can Feel Unbearable

Grief doesn't move in a straight line. Just when you think you're starting to heal, something—a sound, a sight, a familiar moment—can bring everything rushing back. Triggers are powerful because they remind us of what's missing, often in ways we don't expect.

One moment, you're fine. The next, you're **flooded with emotion**—as if the loss just happened all over again. This is normal. It's not a sign that you're "going backward" in your healing journey. **It's a sign of love, memory, and the deep bond you shared with your pet.**

Understanding why triggers happen and how to navigate them can help you regain a sense of balance when grief feels overwhelming.

Sensory Triggers: The Unseen Reminders of Their Presence

Our pets were part of our daily environment, and so much of our grief is tied to **the things they left behind.**

🔊 **Sounds** – The jingle of a collar, the scratch of paws on the floor, or even a similar bark or meow can trigger an intense emotional reaction. For a split second, your brain might trick you into thinking they're still there—until reality sets in.

🛏 **Empty Spaces** – Seeing their **favorite spot**—an untouched bed, an empty space on the couch, or a leash still hanging by the door—can create a deep ache. The absence feels more **visible**, making their loss even more real.

🐾 **Scents & Touch** – Sometimes, it's their lingering scent on a blanket or the feeling of petting another animal with fur like theirs. These sensory triggers can bring comfort, but they can also make grief feel fresh again.

The hardest part? **You can't always prepare for these moments.** They can happen anywhere, at any time, catching you off guard when you least expect it.

Emotional Triggers: The Dates and Moments That Hurt the Most

Some triggers aren't just tied to objects or places—they're tied to **time.** Specific dates or routines can bring an **extra wave of sadness**, especially during the first year without your pet.

Birthdays & Adoption Anniversaries – The days that once marked celebrations can now feel like painful reminders of their absence.

Holidays – Holidays can be particularly tough, especially if your pet was part of your traditions—opening gifts with you, sitting by your feet during family dinners, or simply making the season brighter with their presence.

Daily Routines – Some triggers are more subtle, like **waking up without their greeting, not having them at your side during a quiet evening, or coming home to an empty house**. These everyday moments can be some of the hardest to adjust to.

Knowing these emotional triggers exist **doesn't mean you have to avoid them**—but it helps to acknowledge them and find ways to **honor your pet's memory in a way that brings more love than pain.**

Sudden Waves of Grief: Why Triggers Hit Unexpectedly, Even Years Later

One of the most confusing parts of grief is that just when you think you've found stability, **a trigger can hit out of nowhere—weeks, months, even years later.**

You might be...

- Watching a movie when a scene involving a pet catches you off guard.

- Walking in a park when you see someone with a dog that looks just like yours.

- Having a completely normal day when a memory randomly surfaces, bringing an unexpected rush of tears.

Triggers don't follow a timeline. Even if you've gone **days, weeks, or months without crying,** a single moment can make you feel like you're grieving all over again.

But here's what's important to remember: **This is normal. It doesn't mean you aren't healing.** It means your pet's love is still woven into your heart, and that's okay.

Instead of fighting these moments, **allow them.** Take a deep breath, acknowledge the love behind the sadness, and remind yourself:

"This isn't a setback. This is love, resurfacing in a different way."

Final Thoughts

Triggers are painful, but they are also reminders of **how much your pet meant to you.** They show you that their presence is still alive in your memories, in the routines they left behind, and in the love that never truly fades.

You don't have to avoid triggers—but you can learn how to navigate them with compassion. **Over time, the moments that once brought deep sorrow may also bring comfort.** Instead of being painful reminders of loss, they can become warm reminders of the love that will always remain. 🖤

The Psychological Impact of an Empty Home

The silence after losing a pet is deafening. The house, once filled with their presence—the click of their paws, the rustle of their movements, their quiet companionship—now feels eerily still.

For many pet owners, **home wasn't just a place—it was a shared space filled with the presence of unconditional love.** When that presence is suddenly gone, it can feel like an overwhelming void. The emptiness isn't just physical; it's deeply **psychological and emotional**, affecting the way we move through our daily lives.

Why Loneliness Feels Amplified

Losing a pet is different from other forms of grief because **they were part of your every moment.** Unlike human relationships, which have boundaries and separate spaces, **pets are woven into the fabric of your life in a way that few others are.**

🐾 **They were always there.** Whether you were making coffee, watching TV, or coming home from work, your pet's presence was **a constant source of companionship.**

🐾 **They provided unconditional love.** A pet doesn't judge, hold grudges, or drift away over time. They simply love **fully, without question**, and losing that kind of devotion can feel devastating.

🐾 **They shaped your routine.** From morning feedings to bedtime snuggles, your pet structured your day. Without them, **daily life can feel unfamiliar, like something is permanently missing.**

This is why loneliness after pet loss can feel even more **intense than expected.** It's not just missing *them*—it's missing **the way they made your home feel like home.**

Phantom Sensations: When It Feels Like They're Still There

Many grieving pet owners experience **phantom sensations**—the feeling that their pet is still present, even when they're gone.

🔊 **Hearing familiar sounds** – The soft jingle of a collar, the scratching at the door, the sigh of a pet settling down—only to realize it's just your mind expecting them to still be there.

🐾 **Seeing movement out of the corner of your eye** – A shadow that reminds you of them, a blanket on the floor that, for a split second, looks like they're curled up in their usual spot.

💬 **Feeling their presence** – Some people report feeling a **faint warmth in bed where their pet used to sleep**, or even the sensation of them brushing against their leg.

These experiences can be comforting or unsettling, but they are **a normal part of grief.** Your mind has spent **years recognizing their presence**, and it takes time for it to adjust to their absence.

Rather than fearing these moments, try reframing them as **reminders of the bond you shared.** Your pet was so deeply part of your world that your mind still expects them to be there. **That's love, lingering in the spaces they left behind.**

Guilt Over Adjusting: Why Moving Forward Can Feel Like Betrayal

One of the hardest parts of healing from pet loss is **learning how to adjust without feeling like you're leaving them behind.**

Many people struggle with feelings of guilt when they start to:

- **Feel moments of happiness** without their pet.
- **Stop crying as often.**
- **Change their daily routine** or remove pet-related items from their home.
- **Consider welcoming another pet** in the future.

💔 *"If I move on, does that mean I'm forgetting them?"*

💔 *"Am I replacing them too soon?"*

💔 *"Would they think I don't love them anymore?"*

These thoughts are **completely normal.** But here's the truth:

- **Healing doesn't mean forgetting.** You're not erasing their place in your life—you're learning how to carry their love differently.

- **Your pet would want you to be happy.** The love you shared wasn't about suffering—it was about companionship, joy, and comfort.

- **Moving forward isn't betrayal.** It's a sign that their love helped shape you into someone who still has love to give.

If you're struggling with guilt, try this simple reframe:

Instead of "I'm moving on," try **"I'm carrying them with me as I heal."**

Instead of "I don't need them anymore," try **"They taught me how to love, and I will honor them by continuing to live fully."**

Grief **doesn't mean staying stuck in sorrow.** It means learning how to navigate life in a way that honors their memory while allowing yourself to keep living.

Final Thoughts

An empty home after pet loss isn't just **quiet**—it's **a painful reminder of what's missing.** The loneliness feels amplified, the silence feels unnatural, and adjusting to life without them can feel both heartbreaking and guilt-inducing.

But in time, the emptiness will shift. The quiet will become **softer, less overwhelming.** The guilt will turn into **gratitude for the love you shared.** And your home—though different—will once again feel **like a place filled with love, warmth, and memories that never fade.**

Practical Strategies for Managing Triggers and Adjusting to Change: Creating a New Daily Rhythm Without Forgetting Them

Losing a pet doesn't just leave an emotional void—it disrupts **the entire rhythm of your day.** The routines you built together—morning walks, mealtime rituals, evening snuggles—suddenly disappear, leaving gaps that feel unnatural and painful.

While you can't replace the love and presence of your pet, you can **adjust your daily rhythm in a way that eases emotional pain while keeping their memory close.** Creating new routines, focusing on self-care, and allowing space for both remembrance and healing will help you move forward in a way that feels balanced and authentic.

Finding New Morning and Evening Rituals

Mornings and evenings are often the hardest after losing a pet. **These were the times when they were most present—greeting you when you woke up, curling up beside you at night, following you through your daily routine.** Their absence is deeply felt during these quiet moments.

Rather than letting these times be a source of pain, **gently reshape them into something that brings comfort.**

🏠 **Morning Rituals to Ease the Loss:**

- Start the day with **a small act of remembrance**—lighting a candle, looking at a favorite photo, or whispering, *"Good morning, [pet's name]."*

- Go for a short walk—even if it's just around the block—to keep the habit of starting the day with movement.

- If mornings feel empty, **fill that time with something positive**, like journaling, stretching, or playing soft music.

🌙 **Evening Rituals for Comfort:**

- If your pet used to sleep beside you, place a **special object in their spot**—a favorite blanket, a pillow, or something symbolic of their presence.

- Take a few minutes to **reflect on a happy memory** with them before bed. This can be done through journaling or simply closing your eyes and reliving a favorite moment.

- If nighttime silence feels too heavy, **introduce comforting sounds**, like soft music or nature sounds, to fill the space.

Adjusting your routine doesn't mean **erasing them from your life**—it means creating new rhythms that honor their memory while helping you heal.

Replacing Their Care Routine with Self-Care

One of the biggest challenges after pet loss is **figuring out what to do with the time that was once dedicated to them.** Whether it was feeding them, walking them, grooming them, or simply spending time together, their care was part of your identity.

Instead of letting that time become a painful reminder, **shift it toward self-care**—using it to nurture yourself the way you once nurtured them.

🐾 **If you miss feeding them at a certain time,** use that time to make yourself a nourishing meal or have a cup of tea while reflecting on their love.

🐕 **If you miss your daily walks with them,** continue the habit—walk for your own well-being, letting the movement help process emotions.

📖 **If playtime or snuggle time was your bonding moment,** replace it with something that brings you comfort—reading, meditating, or even volunteering with animals.

Shifting your focus to **self-care doesn't mean forgetting them—it means taking the love and care you gave them and turning some of it inward.**

Acknowledging Their Role in Your Life While Building New Habits

Moving forward after loss isn't about **leaving them behind**—it's about finding **ways to carry their love with you while embracing new experiences.**

✅ **Keep their memory present in small ways.**

- Wear a necklace with their name or keep a framed photo in a special place.
- Say their name out loud when thinking about them—it helps keep their presence alive.

- Share their story with others, keeping their memory alive through conversation.

☑ **Allow yourself to build new habits without guilt.**

- If you're hesitant to start new routines, remind yourself: **Your pet would want you to keep living, not stay stuck in pain.**

- If you're considering adopting another pet one day, **know that opening your heart again doesn't mean replacing them—it means honoring the love they showed you.**

- If something brings you joy, **embrace it.** Healing doesn't mean forgetting—it means learning to love in a new way.

By gradually integrating **small changes and meaningful rituals**, you can reshape your daily life in a way that acknowledges your grief while allowing space for **new moments of healing, growth, and love.**

A Story of Healing: Emma's Morning Tea Ritual

When Emma lost her cat, Whiskers, the hardest part wasn't just the grief—it was the silence. Every morning for ten years, Whiskers had been the first thing she saw when she woke up. He would stretch lazily at the foot of the bed, blink at her with sleepy eyes, then trot to the kitchen, tail flicking, ready for breakfast.

But now, there was no soft paw tapping at her cheek, no gentle purring as she brewed her morning coffee. Just emptiness.

At first, Emma avoided her usual morning routine. She slept in later, skipping breakfast altogether. The quiet of the house felt unbearable, a reminder that Whiskers wasn't there waiting for her anymore.

One morning, as she stood in the kitchen staring at Whiskers' empty food bowl, she felt the grief swell inside her. Instead of pushing it down, she decided to **create a new morning ritual—one that honored Whiskers while helping her heal.**

She put away the food bowl but left a small framed photo of Whiskers on the counter. Then, she made herself a cup of chamomile tea and sat by the window—the same spot where Whiskers used to watch the birds.

As she sipped her tea, she whispered, *Good morning, Whiskers.*

Each morning after that, she continued her new ritual. She would make tea, sit by the window, and take a moment to remember Whiskers—not with overwhelming sadness, but with quiet gratitude.

Over time, her grief softened. The mornings no longer felt hollow. **Instead of focusing on what was missing, she focused on what remained—the love, the memories, and the quiet comfort of knowing Whiskers would always be a part of her heart.**

And so, with each sunrise and each sip of tea, Emma slowly found her way back to herself—one gentle morning at a time.

Final Thoughts

Losing a pet disrupts life in ways we don't always anticipate. **The routines they helped shape don't just disappear overnight, and adjusting to their absence takes time.** But by gently creating **new morning and evening rituals, replacing their care routine with self-care, and finding ways to honor their memory while building new habits,** you can move forward without feeling like you're leaving them behind.

Healing doesn't mean forgetting—it means carrying their love in a way that allows you to keep living, with **a heart forever changed, but never empty.** ♥

Redesigning Spaces to Ease the Pain

After losing a pet, the physical space they once occupied can feel like both a comfort and a source of pain. Their bed sits empty, their favorite toy untouched, their leash still hanging by the door. Each belonging carries a memory, a reminder of their presence—and their absence.

Deciding what to do with their things is deeply personal. **Some people find comfort in keeping everything as it was, while others feel a need to slowly or immediately change their space to ease the pain.** There is no right or wrong way—only what feels most supportive to your healing.

Should You Put Away Their Things?

One of the first decisions many grieving pet owners face is whether to keep, move, or put away their pet's belongings. **There is no set timeline for this—it's entirely up to what feels right for you.**

🐾 **If keeping their things brings comfort...**

- Leave certain items in place until you feel ready to move them.

- Keep a favorite toy or blanket nearby as a source of emotional connection.

- Continue using a special item (like their water bowl) for another pet, if you have one.

🐾 **If seeing their things is too painful...**

- Store them in a safe place for later, rather than making an immediate decision to discard them.

- Move their belongings gradually—one item at a time—as you feel ready.

- If donating feels like the right step, consider giving items to a local animal shelter, where they can bring comfort to another pet in need.

Remember: **You don't have to make any decisions right away.** Healing happens in stages, and what feels unbearable today may feel different weeks or months from now.

Creating a Dedicated Remembrance Space

For those who want to **honor their pet's memory in a meaningful way**, setting up a remembrance space can be a beautiful way to keep them close while allowing for healing.

🐾 **A Memorial Shelf** – Dedicate a small shelf or tabletop to your pet's memory, displaying their photo, collar, paw print, or a favorite toy.

📷 **A Photo Corner** – Frame a favorite picture of them in a special place where you can see it daily, as a way to remember the joy they brought.

🎁 **A Keepsake Box** – If you're not ready to display their things but don't want to part with them, keep a small box with their belongings—something you can revisit when you need to feel close to them.

🌿 **A Living Tribute** – Some people find comfort in **planting a tree or flowers in their honor**, creating a growing memorial that symbolizes their lasting presence.

Having a space that **celebrates their life rather than just marks their absence** can be a powerful way to **move forward while still holding onto the love you shared.**

Gradual vs. Immediate Change: Understanding What Works Best for You

Everyone processes grief differently. Some find that **immediate change**—putting things away, rearranging furniture, or even deep cleaning—helps ease the pain of loss. Others need **a gradual approach**, moving items little by little as they feel ready.

☑ Gradual Change Might Be Best If:

- You feel emotionally attached to their belongings and need time to adjust.

- You want to keep some items in place for comfort but slowly introduce small changes.

- You prefer to revisit their things on your own timeline, without pressure.

☑ Immediate Change Might Be Best If:

- Seeing their things every day is too painful, making it hard to function.

- You feel an urgent need to create a different environment to help you process the loss.

- You know that moving or donating their belongings will bring you a sense of relief rather than regret.

Neither approach is wrong—**only you know what feels right for your healing.** Some people need time to say goodbye, while others find peace in changing their space quickly. **Trust your instincts and allow yourself to grieve at your own pace.**

Final Thoughts

Your home **doesn't have to feel empty just because they're gone.** Whether you choose to keep their belongings, create a remembrance space, or slowly reshape your environment, **the love they brought into your life will always remain.**

Healing isn't about erasing their presence—it's about finding a way to move forward while keeping their memory alive in a way that brings you comfort and peace. ♥

Facing Emotional Triggers Head-On

Grief has a way of sneaking up on you. A familiar smell, an empty space, or even a random memory can trigger **a sudden wave of pain**—sometimes when you least expect it. It might feel unbearable, as if you're reliving the loss all over again.

But avoiding these triggers **only gives them more power**. The key to healing isn't to escape them—it's to **face them with intention, patience, and self-compassion**. By gradually exposing yourself to reminders, practicing mindfulness, and reframing your thoughts, you can navigate grief with more peace and less pain.

How to Desensitize Yourself to Painful Reminders

After losing a pet, even the most ordinary things can feel emotionally overwhelming—seeing their bed, walking past their favorite spot, or even hearing certain sounds that remind you of them. If these triggers feel unbearable, **gentle exposure techniques** can help you regain control over your emotions.

🐾 **Start small.** If you can't bear to look at their bed or collar, place it in a neutral space where you can see it *without forcing yourself to interact with it right away.*

📷 **Look at photos gradually.** If pictures feel too painful, try glancing at one for a few seconds each day. Over time, your brain will associate them not just with loss, but with love and happy memories, too.

📱 **Revisit familiar places when ready.** If taking your usual walking route feels too painful, **start by just driving past the park or standing outside for a moment.** Slowly build up to walking through it again at your own pace.

🎵 **Reintroduce sounds gently.** If certain sounds—like a jingling collar or the scratch of paws on the floor—bring pain, consider **playing recordings of pet sounds softly** in the background to help your brain adjust.

By **gradually reintroducing triggers instead of avoiding them**, you teach your brain that **these reminders are not threats—they are connections to love that still exists.**

The Power of Mindfulness in Grief Moments

When grief hits, the instinct is often to push it away. **But what if, instead of resisting it, you simply sat with it?**

Mindfulness teaches us to **observe emotions without judgment**—to let them come and go without fear of being overwhelmed.

◯ **When sadness arises, acknowledge it.** Instead of thinking, *I can't handle this,* try, *This is grief. This is love. I can sit with this feeling for a moment.*

🪶 **Breathe through the pain.** Take slow, deep breaths—inhale for four counts, hold for four, exhale for four. Let each breath remind you that *grief is a wave that will pass.*

✋ **Name what you're feeling.** Saying *"I feel sad. I feel lonely. I feel lost"* can make emotions less scary, giving you space to process them instead of being consumed by them.

🔔 **Focus on the present.** When a painful memory surfaces, ground yourself by noticing five things around you—the sound of the wind, the feel of your clothes, the warmth of your hands.

Mindfulness doesn't erase grief, but it **teaches you how to sit with it instead of fighting against it**—and in doing so, makes the pain less overwhelming.

Using Affirmations and Positive Reframing

Our thoughts shape our emotions. When we focus only on loss, grief feels **unbearable**. But shifting our perspective—even slightly—can help ease some of the weight we carry.

💬 **Affirmations to reframe grief:**

Instead of **"I lost them forever,"** try **"Their love is still with me, always."**

Instead of **"My life will never be the same,"** try **"Their presence shaped me, and I carry that forward."**

Instead of **"I can't go on without them,"** try **"I am learning to live with their love in a new way."**

🐾 Shifting from pain to gratitude

Grief says: *I lost them too soon.*

Gratitude says: *I was lucky to have them at all.*

Grief says: *I can't handle this pain.*

Gratitude says: *This pain is proof of love that will never fade.*

Grief says: *They're gone.*

Gratitude says: *They changed me, and that can never be lost.*

This doesn't mean denying sadness—it means allowing **love and gratitude** to sit beside it, making grief a little softer.

Final Thoughts

Triggers don't have to control you. By **gently exposing yourself to reminders, practicing mindfulness, and reframing painful thoughts**, you can shift the way grief affects your daily life.

Healing doesn't mean forgetting—it means **learning how to carry your pet's memory with more love than**

pain. And that is something you can do, one small step at a time. ♥

Filling the Void Without Replacing Them: Finding Comfort in Connection

Losing a pet leaves behind an emptiness that's more than just physical—it's emotional, too. **They were your companion, your source of unconditional love, your constant presence.** And when they're gone, it's natural to feel a deep, aching void.

But moving forward doesn't mean *replacing* them. **It means finding new ways to connect—with people, with animals, and with experiences that bring comfort and meaning.**

Rather than isolating yourself in grief, **lean into connection**—with pet-loving friends, support groups, and even animals in need. **Love, when shared, has a way of healing.**

Leaning on Pet-Loving Friends and Family

Not everyone will understand the depth of your grief—but those who **have loved and lost a pet themselves will.** Surrounding yourself with people who truly **get it** can make all the difference.

🐾 **Reach out to pet-loving friends and family.**

- Talk openly about your grief with those who won't minimize your feelings.

- Share stories and memories about your pet—saying their name keeps their presence alive.

- Let others comfort you, even if it's just sitting in silence with someone who understands.

🐾 **Spend time with other animals—without guilt.**

- Being around animals, even if they're not your own, can bring comfort.

- Visit a friend's pet, offer to dog-sit, or simply **enjoy the warmth of animal companionship in a way that feels right for you.**

You don't have to go through this alone. **The love of a pet is special—but so is the support of those who truly understand your loss.**

Joining Pet Loss Support Groups: The Healing Power of Shared Experiences

Sometimes, grief feels isolating—especially if those around you don't fully grasp the depth of your pain. That's where **pet loss support groups** can be invaluable.

💬 **The benefits of connecting with others who've experienced the same loss:**

✅ **Validation** – Knowing you're not alone in your emotions can be incredibly reassuring.

✅ **Safe space to grieve** – No one will tell you to "just move on."

☑ **Guidance from those further along in their healing** – Hearing how others have coped can offer hope and perspective.

🐾 **Where to find support groups:**

- Online communities (Facebook groups, Reddit forums, pet loss websites)

- Local grief counseling centers that offer pet loss support

- Animal shelters or veterinary clinics that host memorial gatherings

Sometimes, the best healing happens **when you share your pain with people who truly understand it.**

Engaging with Animal Rescue or Therapy Programs: Channeling Grief into Meaningful Action

If your grief feels overwhelming, **turning pain into purpose** can be a powerful way to heal. Many people find comfort in **helping other animals in need**, not as a replacement for their pet, but as a way to **honor the love they shared.**

🐾 **Ways to get involved:**

✔ **Volunteer at an animal shelter** – Spending time with shelter pets can bring joy while making a difference.

✔ **Foster an animal in need** – If you're not ready to adopt, fostering provides temporary love to a pet who needs it.

✔ **Support therapy animal programs** – Many hospitals and nursing homes use therapy animals to bring comfort to those in need.

✔ **Donate in your pet's name** – Whether it's food, supplies, or financial aid, giving back is a way to carry their love forward.

Helping another animal doesn't mean you're "moving on." **It means your pet's love is inspiring kindness beyond their time here.**

Final Thoughts

You don't have to face grief alone. **Surround yourself with people who understand, seek support from those who've been through it, and channel your love into something meaningful.**

Filling the void isn't about replacing them—it's about **allowing their love to guide you toward new connections, new purpose, and a healing heart.** 🖤

Introducing Positive Distractions

Grief has a way of taking over. The absence of your pet can feel all-consuming, making it difficult to focus on anything else. While it's important to allow yourself to grieve, it's equally important to **find moments of relief**—not as a way to escape the pain, but as a way to **balance it with moments of light.**

Introducing **positive distractions** can help gently guide your mind toward healing. These aren't about "forgetting"—they're about **rebuilding your world in a way that honors your pet while making space for joy again.**

Exploring New Hobbies or Routines: Finding Activities That Bring Joy Without Guilt

After losing a pet, **daily life feels different**. The routines you once shared with them are now empty spaces in your day. Filling those spaces with **new, meaningful activities** can help create a sense of balance.

🐾 **Try a new hobby** – Whether it's painting, cooking, gardening, or learning a musical instrument, engaging in something new gives your mind a gentle **break from grief.**

🛎 **Change your daily routine** – If mornings or evenings feel especially painful, **introduce small changes**—a new coffee ritual, a morning meditation, or an evening gratitude practice.

📚 **Read books that bring comfort** – Whether it's about pet loss, personal growth, or something completely unrelated, reading can be a form of quiet healing.

It's natural to feel **guilty for enjoying something new** after loss, but remember: **Healing doesn't mean forgetting. It means allowing yourself to keep living, carrying their love with you.**

Volunteering with Animals: A Way to Honor Your Pet's Memory While Helping Others

For many, the love of a pet never truly fades—it just needs a new way to **express itself**. One beautiful way to do this is by helping other animals in need.

🐾 **Volunteer at a shelter** – Walking dogs, playing with cats, or simply providing comfort to animals who need it **can be deeply healing.**

🐾 **Foster a pet** – If you're not ready for another permanent companion, **fostering allows you to provide temporary love and care** to an animal who needs a home.

🐾 **Support therapy animal programs** – Some hospitals, nursing homes, and schools use therapy animals to provide comfort—**a powerful way to share the love your pet gave you.**

🐾 **Donate in their name** – Whether it's food, blankets, or a small financial contribution, giving back **turns grief into kindness.**

Helping another animal **isn't replacing your pet—it's honoring them by spreading the love they taught you.**

Creating a "Grief Journal": Writing Letters to Your Pet as a Way to Process Emotions

Sometimes, the best way to process grief is through **words.** Writing can help **release emotions, express**

love, and bring comfort when the weight of loss feels too heavy.

🖊 **Write letters to your pet** – Tell them about your day, share what you miss about them, or **write down the things you never got to say.**

📖 **Keep a memory journal** – Write down favorite moments, funny stories, and the ways they changed your life. Over time, **this journal will become a collection of love, rather than just loss.**

🖋 **Write as a ritual** – Set aside a few minutes each week to write to them. Whether it's a long letter or just a sentence, **it keeps the connection alive.**

Grief is complex, but **putting it into words makes it feel a little more manageable.**

Final Thoughts

Positive distractions don't mean **ignoring grief**—they mean **allowing yourself to step into small moments of healing** while still holding space for your pet's memory.

Through **new hobbies, volunteering, and writing**, you can **create a balance between sorrow and love**—because healing doesn't mean letting go, it means **finding new ways to carry their love forward.** 🖤

When (and If) to Welcome a New Pet

After losing a beloved pet, the question of welcoming another one can feel overwhelming. Some people feel ready soon after their loss, while others need months or even years before considering it. **There is no right or wrong timeline—only what feels true to your heart.**

Bringing a new pet into your life doesn't mean replacing the one you lost. It's about opening your heart in a way that **honors your past pet while making space for new love.** But before taking that step, it's important to understand your emotions and ensure you're making the decision from a place of **healing, not just longing.**

Understanding Your Emotional Readiness

Grief can make us feel **desperate to fill the emptiness left behind,** but a new pet should never be a quick fix for loss. Before making the decision, ask yourself:

💜 **Am I looking for companionship, or trying to "replace" my pet?**

Grieving is painful, and it's natural to want relief. But if you're hoping a new pet will erase your sadness, **it may be too soon.**

💜 **Does the idea of a new pet bring excitement or guilt?**

If you feel excited about welcoming another pet into your life, it could be a sign that you're emotionally ready. If you feel guilty—like you'd be betraying your pet—it may mean you need more time.

💜 **Am I emotionally strong enough to care for another animal?**

A pet requires time, energy, and love. **If you're still struggling with deep grief, it's okay to wait.** Healing doesn't have to be rushed.

🐾 **Tip:** Instead of making a sudden decision, **spend time around other animals first**—visit a shelter, dog-sit for a friend, or volunteer. **This can help you gauge how ready you feel without pressure.**

Respecting Your Grieving Process

There's **no set timeline** for when (or if) you should adopt another pet. Some people **find comfort in adopting right away**, while others **need years before they're ready**.

✅ If You're Ready Soon:

Some people adopt soon after losing a pet because they thrive on **companionship and routine.** If you feel ready and it brings you peace, **trust that feeling.**

✕ If You Need More Time:

If the thought of another pet feels **too painful or overwhelming**, honor that. **Give yourself permission to grieve at your own pace.**

🐾 **A gentle way to ease in:**

- **Fostering a pet** can be a short-term way to experience companionship without long-term commitment.

- **Volunteering with animals** lets you share love while still healing.

- **Caring for a friend's pet** can help you adjust to being around animals again.

You'll know you're ready when the idea of a new pet **feels like a natural step forward—not an attempt to erase the past.**

How a New Pet Can Complement, Not Replace, the Love You Lost

No two pets are ever the same, and they **shouldn't be.** Each pet has its own personality, quirks, and way of loving.

Bringing a new pet into your life **doesn't mean forgetting the one you lost**—it means allowing their love to **inspire you to open your heart again.**

🐾 **Ways to Honor Your Past Pet While Embracing a New One:**

- **Keep a keepsake** from your past pet—like their collar or photo—to remind you they're always part of your journey.

- **Give your new pet their own identity**—let them be their own unique companion, rather than a "replacement."

- **Use the lessons your past pet taught you**— apply the love, patience, and joy they gave you to your new furry friend.

💚 **Love is infinite.** Adopting a new pet isn't about moving on—it's about moving forward **with the love of your past pet still in your heart.**

A Story of Remembrance: Lucy's Evening Porch Light

For ten years, every evening after dinner, Emily and her golden retriever, Lucy, would sit together on the front porch. It was their quiet ritual—Emily with her cup of tea, Lucy curled up beside her, watching the world settle down for the night.

When Lucy passed away, the porch felt unbearably empty. The first evening without her, Emily stepped outside and instinctively reached down to run her fingers through Lucy's fur—only to be met with nothing but air. The silence was suffocating.

For weeks, she avoided the porch altogether. It felt wrong to sit there alone, as if continuing the routine without Lucy would be some kind of betrayal. But as the days passed, she realized that avoiding it didn't make the pain go away—it only made Lucy's absence feel stronger.

One evening, Emily stepped outside again, carrying Lucy's worn collar in her pocket. She turned on the porch light and whispered, *"I miss you, Lu."*

That night, a new ritual was born.

Every evening, Emily made a point to **turn on the porch light in Lucy's honor.** It became her way of saying, *"I remember you. You're still with me."* Some nights, she sat for a few moments, sipping tea, letting the memories wash over her. Other nights, she simply flipped the switch, offering a quiet nod to the night, feeling a sense of warmth in the gesture.

Over time, the pain softened. The porch light was no longer just about loss—it was about love, about remembrance, about keeping their bond alive in a way that felt peaceful instead of painful.

And every evening, as Emily illuminated the porch, she imagined Lucy beside her, tail wagging in approval, still keeping her company in the way that only a beloved companion could.

Final Thoughts

Deciding whether to welcome a new pet is **a deeply personal choice.** If and when you do, let it be from a place of **love, not just loss.**

Your pet would want you to be happy. They would want you to love again—not to replace them, but to **continue the incredible bond you once shared.**

And when the time feels right, **your heart will know.**

Chapter Summary: Adjusting to Life After Pet Loss

The **daily void** left after losing a pet is one of the hardest parts of grief. It's not just the emotional pain—it's the disruption of routines, the empty spaces in your home, and the absence of their comforting presence.

But **healing doesn't mean forgetting**. It means **learning how to coexist with the loss** in a way that allows you to cherish their memory without being consumed by grief. Small, intentional actions—whether it's creating a remembrance space, adjusting your routines, or finding meaningful ways to honor them—can help you **move forward while keeping their love close.**

Action Step:

Choose **one space in your home or daily routine** that feels especially empty without your pet. **Create a small ritual** to honor them—whether it's lighting a candle, displaying a photo, or dedicating a moment of gratitude each day. **These small acts of remembrance can bring comfort as you navigate life after loss.** 🖤

CHAPTER 5

Honoring Your Pet's Memory in a Meaningful Way

"The love of a pet never truly leaves us. It lives on in the stories we tell, the lessons they taught us, and the ways we choose to honor their memory."

After a pet passes, many people struggle with how to keep their memory alive without feeling stuck in grief. Creating rituals, memorials, and meaningful traditions can be a powerful way to celebrate their life while allowing yourself to heal. This chapter will explore unique, heartfelt ways to honor your pet, ensuring their love and legacy live on.

Why Memorializing Your Pet Helps the Healing Process: The Psychological Benefits of Memorialization

Losing a pet leaves an undeniable void, one that isn't just emotional but deeply woven into the routines and moments of daily life. In the midst of grief, it can feel overwhelming to move forward while still honoring the love you shared. This is where **memorialization** plays a powerful role—it transforms pain into purpose, provides closure without erasure, and helps keep your pet's spirit alive in a meaningful way.

Memorializing your pet isn't about "moving on" or leaving them behind—it's about creating **a lasting tribute that acknowledges their impact while allowing you to heal.**

Helps Process Grief in a Structured Way: Turning Pain into Meaningful Action

Grief can feel chaotic, unpredictable, and deeply isolating. **Creating a memorial provides structure—a tangible way to work through emotions and channel grief into action.**

🐾 **Memorialization gives grief a focus.** Whether it's making a scrapbook, planting a tree, or writing letters to your pet, having a **dedicated project** can help process emotions in a healthy, intentional way.

🐾 **It provides a sense of purpose.** Instead of feeling lost in sorrow, creating a tribute helps turn **love into action**—ensuring that their memory is preserved in a way that feels comforting.

🐾 **It allows for expression.** Some grief is too heavy for words, but memorials offer **an alternative form of expression**—through art, storytelling, or meaningful rituals that help release emotions over time.

By **giving your grief direction**, memorializing becomes an important step toward healing—one that allows you to process your loss without feeling like you're leaving your pet behind.

Provides a Sense of Closure Without Forgetting: Honoring Their Impact While Moving Forward

One of the hardest parts of pet loss is **the fear of forgetting**—the worry that, as time passes, their presence will fade. A memorial serves as a gentle reassurance that **they will always be part of your story.**

🕯 **Closure doesn't mean goodbye—it means transformation.** Instead of holding onto pain, a memorial allows you to **shift grief into remembrance, love, and gratitude.**

🖼 **Honoring them helps integrate their memory into your life.** Whether through a photo display, a dedicated space in your home, or a personal ritual, these acts **keep their presence alive in a way that brings comfort, not just sadness.**

🪶 **Memorials create a lasting legacy.** Even small acts—like lighting a candle on special days, keeping a keepsake, or donating to an animal shelter in their name—become **living testaments to the love you shared.**

Memorialization doesn't erase grief, but **it allows healing to take shape in a way that feels right for you.**

Strengthens Emotional Connection: Keeping Their Spirit Alive in Your Heart

Love doesn't end when life does. **Memorializing your pet helps keep the emotional connection strong,**

allowing you to cherish their presence even after they're gone.

💜 **It turns pain into love.** When grief feels overwhelming, small acts of remembrance—like saying their name, visiting a favorite place, or holding onto a meaningful item—help keep the love alive in a gentle, healing way.

🐶 **It reminds you of the joy they brought.** Instead of focusing only on loss, a memorial shifts the focus to **celebrating their life, their quirks, their unconditional love.**

🐾 **It allows you to carry them forward.** Grief may soften, but love remains. Memorializing your pet isn't about holding onto the past—it's about **bringing their love into your future in a way that feels peaceful and meaningful.**

Final Thoughts

Memorializing your pet isn't just about creating something physical—it's about **giving your grief a home, a direction, a way to transform pain into love.**

By choosing to honor them in a meaningful way, you allow yourself to heal while ensuring their presence stays with you—not just in memory, but in the way they shaped your heart forever. 💜

Understanding Personal vs. Shared Memorials

Memorializing a pet is deeply personal. Some people find comfort in **quiet, private remembrance**, while others feel supported by **sharing their grief with a community.** There's no right or wrong way—only what feels most healing to you.

Understanding the difference between personal and shared memorials can help you decide how you'd like to honor your pet in a way that brings comfort and meaning.

Personal Memorials: Quiet, Private Ways to Remember Your Pet

Some people prefer to grieve **in solitude**, finding peace in quiet moments of reflection. A personal memorial is something **just for you**—a way to privately honor your pet in a meaningful way.

🐾 **Ideas for Personal Memorials:**

🪶 **Create a home tribute** – Set up a small space with their photo, collar, or a candle to keep their presence close.

📖 **Write letters to your pet** – Express what you miss, what they meant to you, and how their love changed your life.

🎶 **Make a special playlist** – Collect songs that remind you of them and listen when you want to feel close to their memory.

🌳 **Plant a tree or flowers in their honor** – Watching something grow can symbolize the continuation of their love.

🕯 **Light a candle on special days** – Birthdays, adoption anniversaries, or simply days when you need comfort.

A **personal memorial allows for quiet healing**—a way to grieve at your own pace without external pressure.

Community Memorials: Engaging in Shared Grief Through Group Remembrance

For some, **grief feels lighter when shared**. Community memorials offer **a way to connect with others who understand**, allowing you to honor your pet while feeling supported by those who have experienced similar loss.

🐾 **Ways to Participate in Community Memorials:**

📅 **Join a pet remembrance event** – Some shelters, veterinary clinics, and grief support groups hold memorial gatherings where pet owners can share stories and honor their companions together.

🐶 **Contribute to a pet memorial wall** – Many animal organizations offer digital or physical spaces where people can post tributes and photos of their pets.

💜 **Donate or sponsor an animal in their name** – Supporting a shelter or rescue in your pet's memory allows their love to live on through helping another animal in need.

📣 **Join an online pet loss support group** – Sometimes, simply sharing your pet's story with others who understand can bring comfort.

Community memorials provide **connection and validation**, reminding you that you're not alone in your grief.

Balancing Both Approaches: Finding What Feels Right for Your Healing Journey

Some people prefer **a deeply personal remembrance**, while others find strength in **grieving alongside a community**. But you don't have to choose just one— **many people find comfort in a combination of both.**

💜 **Ask yourself:**

- Do I feel more comforted by **solitude or shared connection**?
- Would I like to honor my pet privately, or **do I want to share their memory with others**?
- Would a community memorial help me feel **less alone in my grief**?

🐾 **You might choose to...**

- Keep a **private remembrance space** at home while also participating in a **shared pet loss event**.

- Write **personal letters to your pet** but also join an **online support group** to hear others' experiences.

- Create a **memorial garden at home** and **plant a tree in their honor at a park or animal shelter.**

Grief is unique to every person, and so is the way we choose to **remember those we've lost.**

Final Thoughts

Whether you choose a **personal, shared, or blended approach**, the most important thing is that your memorial feels **authentic to your love for your pet.**

Honor them in a way that brings you comfort—because **their love was unique, and so is the way you carry it forward.** ♥

When Grief Becomes Unhealthy Memorialization

Memorializing your pet is a powerful way to **honor their love and keep their memory alive**, but sometimes grief can take a turn where remembrance **starts holding you back instead of helping you heal.**

It's important to recognize the difference between **healthy memorialization**, which brings comfort and connection, and **unhealthy grief**, which keeps you stuck in pain. **Healing doesn't mean forgetting—it means finding a balance where you can honor their memory while still living fully.**

Clinging vs. Honoring: Recognizing When Memorials Hold You Back

Memorials should be a **source of comfort, not a barrier to moving forward**. While it's natural to hold onto your pet's memory, **there is a point where grief stops being healing and starts becoming a weight.**

💜 **Signs You May Be Clinging to Grief Instead of Honoring Their Memory:**

▶ **You feel guilty for experiencing joy.** If you catch yourself thinking, *"I shouldn't be happy without them,"* it may be a sign you're clinging to grief instead of carrying their love forward.

▶ **You can't bring yourself to change anything.** If you're unable to move their belongings, avoiding rooms they spent time in, or resisting even small adjustments, grief may be keeping you frozen.

▶ **Your memorial feels like a shrine to loss rather than a celebration of life.** Instead of bringing warmth, does it only bring sadness? If so, it may need to be reframed into something that brings peace instead of pain.

🐾 **Healthy memorialization allows you to feel close to your pet while still embracing the present.** If your remembrance rituals **bring only sorrow**, it may be time to rethink their role in your healing process.

Feeling Guilty for 'Moving On': Healing Does Not Mean Forgetting

One of the biggest emotional struggles in grief is **the guilt of moving forward.** Many pet owners feel a **sense of betrayal** if they begin to experience happiness again or if they consider welcoming another pet into their life.

💬 **Common Thoughts That Signal Guilt:**

- *"If I stop feeling sad, does that mean I didn't love them enough?"*

- *"If I put away their things, does that mean I'm erasing them?"*

- *"If I bond with another pet, does that mean they didn't matter?"*

But here's the truth: **Moving forward doesn't mean leaving them behind—it means carrying their love with you in a new way.**

✅ **You don't have to 'let go' to heal.** Love doesn't disappear, and neither does their impact on your life.

✅ **Healing means integrating their memory into your future, not erasing it from your past.**

✅ **Your pet would want you to be happy.** They would never want you to suffer forever because of their absence.

Instead of thinking of it as "moving on," **think of it as moving forward—with them still in your heart.**

Finding a Balance: Honoring Their Memory Without Staying Trapped in the Past

The goal is to **find a balance between remembrance and growth**—where you can cherish their memory while still allowing yourself to **live fully in the present.**

🐾 **Healthy Ways to Keep Their Memory Alive Without Holding Yourself Back:**

✔ **Reframe your memorial into a source of comfort.** Adjust it so that it brings warmth and gratitude instead of only sadness.

✔ **Allow yourself to embrace joy again.** Laugh at old memories, share their story, and recognize that happiness does not diminish their significance.

✔ **When ready, introduce small changes.** You don't have to put everything away at once, but gently adjusting your space can be part of the healing process.

✔ **Know that your love is not measured by how long you grieve.** You can honor them **while still allowing yourself to move forward.**

Healing is not about forgetting—it's about **finding a way to carry their love with you in a way that brings you peace, not pain.**

Final Thoughts

Memorials should be a bridge between **grief and healing,** not a chain that keeps you stuck in sorrow. If you find yourself **clinging to pain instead of embracing their love**, it may be time to reframe how you honor them.

Your pet **wouldn't want you to live in sadness forever**—they would want you to remember them with love, gratitude, and the joy they brought into your life. 💙

Unique and Personalized Ways to Honor Your Pet: Creating a Lasting Tribute

Every pet leaves behind a unique imprint on our hearts, and **the way we honor them should be just as special as the love we shared**. A lasting tribute doesn't have to be elaborate—it just needs to be **meaningful to you**. Whether it's creating a small remembrance space, planting something in their honor, or wearing a keepsake that carries their spirit, these personal touches help keep their memory alive in a way that brings **comfort, warmth, and connection**.

Memorial Spaces at Home: A Tribute That Feels Close

Sometimes, just having a **dedicated space** to honor your pet can bring a sense of peace. A home tribute is a simple but powerful way to **create a space where their presence is always felt**.

🐾 Ideas for a Memorial Space:

📷 **Photo Shrine** – Arrange your favorite pictures of them on a shelf or table, perhaps with their collar, paw print, or a small candle.

🎁 **Keepsake Box** – Store special items like their tag, a favorite toy, or even letters you've written to them.

🪔 **Tribute Corner** – Set up a small space with flowers, a memory candle, or a framed quote that reminds you of their love.

A home tribute doesn't have to be big—it just has to be a space where you can feel their presence.

Planting a Tree or Garden in Their Honor: A Living, Growing Reminder

A beautiful way to honor your pet is by creating something **that continues to grow, just like the love you shared.**

🌳 **Plant a Tree in Their Name** – Watching a tree grow year after year can be a comforting reminder that **love never truly fades—it just changes form.** Choose a spot in your yard or a meaningful location, and dedicate it to your pet's memory.

🌼 **Create a Memorial Garden** – Whether it's a single flower pot or a full garden, planting flowers in their honor can provide a space of reflection and peace. You can even place a small memorial stone with their name in the garden.

💜 **Symbolic Plants** – Some flowers and trees carry meaning that can reflect your pet's spirit:

- **Forget-Me-Nots** – A symbol of remembrance.
- **Sunflowers** – Represent warmth and joy, just like the happiness your pet brought.

- **Oak Tree** – Symbolizes strength and the lasting impact of their love.

A living tribute ensures that their memory continues to thrive, bringing beauty and life to the world they left behind.

Custom Artwork or Jewelry: Keeping Their Spirit Close

For those who find comfort in **having something tangible to hold onto**, personalized art or jewelry can be a meaningful tribute.

🎨 **Commission a Custom Painting or Portrait** – A beautiful way to celebrate their life, whether as a realistic painting or an abstract piece that captures their essence.

💎 **Wear a Keepsake in Their Memory** –

- **Necklaces or bracelets with their name or paw print**
- **Lockets with a tiny photo or a piece of their fur inside**
- **Custom rings or charms engraved with a special message**

🐾 **Turn Their Paw Print into Art** – If you have their paw print, you can turn it into a framed piece, a tattoo, or even a piece of engraved jewelry.

Carrying a piece of them with you—whether through art, jewelry, or something symbolic—can

serve as a constant reminder that their love is always with you.

Final Thoughts

Memorials don't have to be traditional—they just have to be **personal**. Whether it's a **photo tribute, a living garden, or a wearable keepsake**, creating a lasting tribute helps **transform grief into something meaningful**—a reminder that the love you shared **continues, in new and beautiful ways.** ♥

Keeping Their Memory Alive in Everyday Life

The love of a pet doesn't fade with time—it continues to live in the small moments, the memories that resurface unexpectedly, and the habits they helped shape. **Keeping their memory alive isn't just about grand gestures—it's about weaving their presence into your everyday life in ways that bring you comfort and connection.**

By carrying a keepsake, writing letters, or creating a digital tribute, you can ensure that your pet's legacy **remains a cherished part of your journey** while allowing yourself to heal.

Carrying a Small Keepsake with You: A Tangible Reminder of Their Love

Sometimes, the smallest things bring the greatest comfort. Carrying a **small token** that reminds you of your pet can make their presence feel close, even as you move forward.

🐾 Meaningful Keepsake Ideas:

💙 **Locket with their photo** – A simple way to keep them near your heart.

🔑 **Keychain or engraved tag** – Many people repurpose their pet's collar tag into a keychain or engrave their name on a small charm.

🔗 **Wearable tribute** – Rings, bracelets, or necklaces with their paw print, name, or a special quote.

🐶 **Carrying a small token from them** – A small tuft of fur in a keepsake vial, a piece of their favorite blanket, or even their leash tucked inside your bag for comfort.

Having a **physical reminder** of your pet can offer moments of reassurance, allowing their presence to **stay close even as life moves forward.**

Writing Letters to Your Pet: A Journaling Technique for Ongoing Healing

Grief doesn't end after a certain amount of time—it evolves. And sometimes, **continuing the conversation** with your pet can be incredibly healing. Writing letters to them allows you to express emotions, share memories, and maintain a connection.

✍️ How to Write a Letter to Your Pet:

✉️ **Tell them what you miss.** Share the little things—like their wagging tail, their happy purr, or the way they made bad days better.

✉️ **Update them on your life.** Talk to them as if they're still listening. *"I saw a dog today that reminded me of you, and it made me smile."*

✉️ **Express your gratitude.** Let them know how much they meant to you and how they shaped your life.

✉️ **Say what you need to say.** If you carry any guilt, regrets, or emotions that feel unresolved, writing them down can help bring closure.

Writing letters doesn't mean **clinging to the past**—it's a way to **honor the bond you shared and allow healing to unfold naturally.**

Creating a Digital Memory Book or Video Montage: Sharing Their Story with Loved Ones

In today's world, digital memorials are a beautiful way to celebrate your pet's life and share their story with those who loved them too.

📱 Ideas for a Digital Tribute:

📷 **Create a memory book** – Use a digital photo album or scrapbook app to collect pictures, funny moments, and heartfelt captions.

📽 **Make a video montage** – Compile clips of your pet set to a meaningful song and watch it whenever you need a comforting reminder of their love.

🖥 **Start a tribute page or post on social media** – Sharing their story with others can bring support and allow their memory to live on.

⬤ **Donate or sponsor an animal in their name** – Many animal organizations allow you to dedicate a donation in honor of a pet, creating a **living tribute** that helps other animals in need.

Whether it's a **photo slideshow, a written reflection, or a digital scrapbook**, creating a memory keeps their spirit alive—not just in your heart, but in the hearts of others who loved them too.

Final Thoughts

Keeping your pet's memory alive isn't about **holding onto grief—it's about carrying their love forward in a way that feels meaningful to you.** Whether through a small keepsake, heartfelt letters, or a digital tribute, these acts of remembrance ensure that their presence remains **a cherished part of your everyday life.** ♥

Giving Back in Their Name

One of the most beautiful ways to honor a beloved pet is to **channel your grief into positive action.** The love they gave you doesn't have to end with their passing—it can continue to **make a difference in the lives of other animals** who need love, care, and a second chance.

Giving back in your pet's name is not about replacing them; it's about **keeping their spirit alive through acts of kindness.** Whether through donations, volunteering, or starting a pet-related project, you can turn sorrow into a **lasting tribute that helps others—just as your pet once helped you.**

Donating to an Animal Rescue or Shelter: Turning Grief into Positive Action

Many pets in shelters **don't have the love and security** that your pet was lucky to experience. **Making a donation in your pet's honor** is a meaningful way to give back while ensuring their memory contributes to something good.

🐾 **Ways to Donate in Their Name:**

✔ **Monetary Donations** – Give to a local shelter, rescue, or national pet charity that aligns with your pet's story.

✔ **Supply Donations** – Donate blankets, food, toys, or medical supplies to a shelter. Some places have wish lists where you can choose exactly what's needed.

✔ **Sponsor an Animal** – Many rescues offer sponsorship programs where you can cover the costs of an animal's care in honor of your pet.

✔ **Create a Memorial Fundraiser** – If your pet's story inspires others, you can create an online fundraiser for a shelter or rescue that needs support.

💔 **How It Helps You Heal:**

Giving back helps **turn pain into purpose**, allowing your pet's love to **extend beyond their time with you** and touch the lives of animals in need.

Volunteering with Animals: Finding Comfort Through Helping Other Pets

If you're not ready to adopt another pet but miss **the companionship of animals**, volunteering can be a powerful way to **heal while making a difference.**

🐶 **Ways to Volunteer in Your Pet's Honor:**

✔ **Walk shelter dogs** – Give them the love and exercise they desperately need.

✔ **Cuddle or socialize cats** – Many rescues need volunteers to help shy or nervous cats feel comfortable.

✔ **Assist with adoption events** – Help other pets find their forever homes.

✔ **Foster an animal in need** – Provide temporary care for a pet, offering love and safety while they wait for adoption.

💚 **Why It's Healing:**

- Being around animals can **soothe grief and provide comfort** without the commitment of a new pet.

- It gives you a way to **honor your pet's memory through direct action.**

- It helps create a **legacy of love**—ensuring that the care your pet received is extended to other animals in need.

Starting a Small Pet-Related Project: Turning Love into a Legacy

For those who want to do something special in their pet's name, starting a **pet-related project** can be a lasting way to celebrate their impact.

🐾 **Ideas for a Meaningful Project:**

💜 **Fundraiser for a Shelter or Vet Clinic** – Host an event, an online campaign, or a donation drive in memory of your pet.

📢 **Raise Awareness for Pet Adoption** – Share your pet's story to inspire others to adopt instead of shop.

🐾 **Sponsor a Pet Park Bench or Memorial Plaque** – Some parks or shelters allow you to **dedicate a space** in your pet's honor.

🎁 **Create Comfort Kits for Shelter Pets** – Assemble care packages with blankets, treats, and toys for animals waiting for homes.

HOW TO OVERCOME PET LOSS, GRIEF & BEGIN HEALING

💬 **Start a Pet Grief Support Group** – Help others who are struggling with loss by creating a safe space for healing.

💡 **Why It Matters:**

These projects **turn grief into action**, giving your pet's love a **continued purpose**. Every small act of kindness spreads their memory further, ensuring they **continue to make a difference in the world.**

A Story of Giving: Charlie's Legacy

When Megan lost Charlie, her loyal Labrador, the house felt empty in a way she couldn't put into words. For twelve years, Charlie had been her best friend—always at her side, always ready with a wagging tail and warm eyes that made even the hardest days easier.

In the first few weeks after his passing, Megan struggled to find purpose. His food bowl sat untouched in the corner, his favorite blanket still lay draped over the couch, and every time she walked through the front door, she expected to hear the familiar sound of his paws rushing to greet her.

One evening, while scrolling through her phone, Megan came across an article about a local animal shelter that was in desperate need of supplies. She hesitated for a moment, then glanced at Charlie's leash hanging by the door. **Maybe, just maybe, she could turn her grief into something meaningful.**

The next morning, she packed up a box filled with Charlie's unused toys, extra food, and blankets—items he had loved and ones she had bought for him just weeks before he passed. With a deep breath, she drove to the shelter.

As she walked in, the sounds of barking and meowing filled the space, bringing an unexpected sense of comfort. A staff member greeted her warmly, and as Megan explained that she was donating in **Charlie's name**, she felt an unexpected lump in her throat.

"We actually have a new rescue who reminds me a lot of him," the staff member said, leading her to one of the kennels. Inside, a golden-eyed Labrador mix sat quietly, his tail wagging hesitantly as their eyes met.

Megan knelt down, smiling through the tears. **Charlie had been loved every single day of his life, and now, in his honor, another dog would have the same chance.**

That day, she left the shelter feeling lighter. She knew she wasn't ready for another dog just yet, but she also knew that **Charlie's love hadn't ended—it had simply found a new way to live on.**

From that day forward, every year on Charlie's birthday, Megan returned to the shelter with donations—treats, blankets, food, and toys—all labeled with a simple tag:

"In loving memory of Charlie, who was loved beyond words."

And in giving back, she realized something beautiful: **Charlie's legacy wasn't just in the past. It was in every wagging tail, every rescued heart, and every act of love that carried his spirit forward.** 🖤

Final Thoughts

Giving back in your pet's name **doesn't erase grief, but it transforms it**—allowing their love to live on in the lives they touch. Whether it's through **donating, volunteering, or starting a meaningful project**, you can create a lasting tribute that reflects the bond you shared.

Because **love like theirs doesn't end—it just finds new ways to shine.** 🖤

Special Rituals to Honor Their Life: Annual Remembrance Traditions

Grief may soften over time, but **love never fades**. Finding ways to honor your pet's life through annual traditions can bring comfort, keep their memory alive, and turn sorrow into a celebration of the love you shared.

Whether it's **lighting a candle, gathering loved ones, or visiting a favorite place**, these rituals ensure that your pet's presence remains a cherished part of your life—not just in memory, but in action.

Lighting a Candle on Important Dates: Keeping Their Memory Alive with Intention

Some days hold **extra significance**—their adoption anniversary, birthday, or the day they passed. Lighting a candle on these dates **creates a sacred moment** to remember them with love.

🕯 How to Create a Candle Ritual:

- Choose a special candle that represents them—maybe a color that reminds you of their fur or a scent that brings comfort.

- Light it on significant days, take a deep breath, and reflect on a favorite memory.

- Say their name, whisper a message to them, or simply sit in the quiet warmth of remembrance.

This simple act **turns grief into presence**, allowing you to honor their life with love rather than only sadness.

Holding a Yearly Celebration of Their Life: Sharing Memories with Loved Ones

Your pet wasn't just special to you—**they were part of your family, your circle, your story.** Bringing people together to share memories is a beautiful way to **celebrate the joy they brought into the world.**

🎉 Ways to Celebrate Their Life:

🐾 Host a small gathering with friends and family who knew them. Share stories, look through photos, or even enjoy their favorite treats together.

🐾 Cook a meal in their honor—maybe the foods they always begged for or a recipe inspired by them.

🐾 Create a "memory jar" where everyone writes down a favorite moment or something they loved about your pet.

🐾 Donate to an animal shelter in their name or bring gifts (food, blankets, toys) to a rescue on their remembrance day.

By turning their memory into **a celebration rather than just a loss**, you ensure their love continues to bring people together.

Revisiting Their Favorite Places: Keeping Their Spirit Alive in Meaningful Spaces

Some places feel **like home because of the memories tied to them**—a park where they ran freely, a beach where they chased waves, or a cozy spot in the house where they always curled up beside you.

🪶 How to Honor Them Through Special Places:

🐾 Visit their favorite park or trail and take a quiet walk in their honor. Imagine them by your side, just as they always were.

🐾 If they loved the beach, let the waves carry your thoughts to them—write their name in the sand, knowing the ocean will take your love further.

🐾 If they had a favorite sunny spot in the house, place a plant or a small memorial item there, letting it continue to be **their space.**

Going to these places isn't about **reliving loss—it's about feeling close to them in the places that made them happiest.**

Final Thoughts

Rituals aren't just about **remembering the past—they're about keeping love alive in the present.** By lighting a candle, sharing stories, or revisiting cherished places, you create **a bridge between memory and healing.**

Because love like theirs **never really leaves—it just finds new ways to shine.** 🖤

Spiritual and Symbolic Practices: Honoring Your Pet Through Meaningful Rituals

Grief is not just emotional—it's deeply spiritual for many people. Finding **symbolic ways to honor your pet** can bring a sense of peace, connection, and continued love. Whether through **writing messages, creating a lasting tribute, or engaging in meditation or prayer**, these practices allow you to express your emotions in a **sacred and intentional way.**

Writing a Message and Releasing It: Letting Go with Love

Sometimes, we hold onto words left unspoken—**things we wish we could say, gratitude we didn't express enough, or just a simple "I miss you."** Writing these thoughts down and releasing them into the world can be a powerful way to **symbolically send love to your pet.**

📨 Ways to Release a Message:

🔖 **Balloons (Biodegradable Only)** – Write a note and release it into the sky, watching it rise as a symbol of your love reaching them.

🌊 **Paper Boats** – Write a message, fold it into a small boat, and set it afloat on a river or lake as a symbolic journey.

🎐 **Biodegradable Lanterns** – Light a paper lantern and release it at dusk, letting the warm glow carry your words into the night.

🔥 **Burning a Letter** – Write a heartfelt letter and safely burn it, imagining the smoke as a bridge between you and your pet.

Why It Helps:

- Provides a **sense of closure and release** for lingering emotions.

- Creates a **ritual of connection**, allowing you to send love even after they're gone.

- Helps shift grief into a **moment of peace**, knowing your words are carried to them in some way.

Creating a Memory Stone: A Lasting Tribute in Nature

A **memory stone** is a beautiful way to **keep your pet's presence close**, whether in a garden, on a trail, or in a meaningful space. Engraving their name into a stone or painting a special rock creates **a lasting tribute**—one that stands the test of time.

❀ Ways to Create a Memory Stone:

✐ Paint a smooth rock – Decorate it with their name, a paw print, or a quote that reminds you of them.

☐ Engrave their name into a stone – Place it in your garden, by their favorite spot, or in a peaceful outdoor space.

🌱 Bury a stone beneath a tree – Planting a tree and placing a memory stone beneath it symbolizes **growth and the continuation of love.**

⚑ Leave a stone on a trail or park bench – Mark a spot where you and your pet shared happy times.

Why It Helps:

- Gives you **a physical place to visit and reflect.**

- Creates a **permanent, natural memorial** that keeps their presence alive.

- Allows you to **connect with them through nature**, where love and energy never fade.

Meditation or Prayer in Their Honor: Finding Peace Through Spiritual Connection

For many, grief is **as much a spiritual journey as it is an emotional one**. Taking time to meditate, pray, or engage in quiet reflection can help bring **a sense of comfort, connection, and healing.**

🕊 Ways to Meditate or Pray in Their Honor:

☐ **Guided Meditation** – Close your eyes, take deep breaths, and visualize your pet happy, free, and still with you in spirit.

🪶 **Prayer or Blessing** – If prayer brings comfort, dedicate a few moments each day to say their name and express gratitude for their love.

🕯 **Light a Candle in Meditation** – Sit in a quiet space, light a candle, and simply **be with their memory** in stillness.

🎵 **Use Music or Nature Sounds** – Playing soft music or nature sounds while reflecting on their love can bring **a deep sense of peace.**

Why It Helps:

- Provides a **calm, intentional space** for remembrance.

- Helps process emotions in a **gentle, non-verbal way.**

- Strengthens the **spiritual bond** you shared, reminding you that love never truly disappears.

Final Thoughts

Spiritual and symbolic rituals help us **bridge the gap between grief and connection**, allowing us to **honor, release, and carry love forward** in ways that feel sacred and intentional.

Whether you **release a message, create a lasting tribute in nature, or engage in meditation or prayer,** these acts of remembrance **transform loss into a continued bond—one that exists beyond time, space, and sorrow.** 🖤

Legacy Projects: Keeping Their Spirit Alive for Future Generations

Our pets may leave this world, but **their impact on our hearts is forever.** The love they gave, the lessons they taught, and the memories they created deserve to be carried forward. **Legacy projects allow you to keep their spirit alive, not just for yourself, but for future generations who can learn from and be inspired by their story.**

Whether through **writing, sharing their journey online, or opening your heart to another pet,** these projects ensure that their love **continues to make a difference.**

Compiling a Pet Memoir: Preserving Their Story Through Writing

Every pet has a story, and writing it down **ensures that their memory never fades.** A pet memoir isn't just about capturing their life—it's about **honoring the moments, quirks, and love that made them special.**

📖 How to Create a Pet Memoir:

📷 **Gather Photos** – Arrange them in a timeline or a scrapbook, highlighting their happiest moments.

📝 **Write Down Memories** – Funny habits, favorite spots, and heartwarming stories.

📩 **Include Letters to Your Pet** – Express what they meant to you, the lessons they taught, and how they changed your life.

💬 **Ask Others to Share Stories** – Family and friends may have their own favorite memories of your pet that you can include.

🐾 **Bonus Idea: Turn your memoir into a printed book** to keep on your shelf or share with loved ones. Some even create illustrated children's books **inspired by their pet's life.**

Why It Helps:

- Gives their story a **permanent place in history**.
- Allows you to relive happy moments with love instead of only grief.
- Provides comfort to others who knew and loved them.

Creating an Online Tribute Page: Sharing Their Legacy with Others

In the digital age, sharing a pet's story online **creates a lasting tribute that others can visit, interact with, and draw comfort from.** It also allows those who knew your pet to **contribute their own memories, photos, and messages.**

🌐 **Ways to Share Their Legacy Online:**

🐾 **Create a Memorial Website** – A dedicated page with their photos, story, and a place for others to leave messages.

📱 **Social Media Tribute** – A post or ongoing page where you can share memories, milestones, or lessons they taught you.

🎞 **Video Montage** – A compilation of video clips, photos, and music to celebrate their life.

💜 **Pet Memorial Groups** – Many online communities offer virtual spaces where people can share stories and support one another in their grief.

Why It Helps:

- Keeps their memory **accessible and interactive** for family, friends, and even strangers who relate to their story.

- Provides a **source of comfort** when you want to revisit their presence.

- Offers **connection with others** who understand pet loss and can share in your love for them.

Passing on Their Love to a New Pet: A Continuation, Not a Replacement

One of the greatest ways to honor a pet's legacy is to **continue the love they gave you by opening your**

heart to another pet. This doesn't mean replacing them—**it means carrying forward the kindness, joy, and care they brought into your life.**

🐶 **Ways to Pass on Their Love:**

- **Adopting or fostering a pet in need** when you're ready.

- **Naming a new pet after them or in their honor**—either directly or with a subtle nod to their memory.

- **Using the lessons they taught you** to become an even better pet guardian in the future.

- **Donating supplies, food, or resources** to animals in need, ensuring that other pets get to experience the same love yours did.

Why It Helps:

- Transforms grief into **something positive and life-giving**.

- Ensures that your pet's impact **doesn't end with their passing**.

- Reminds you that **love isn't finite—there's always room for more.**

When the time is right, welcoming another pet **isn't about moving on—it's about moving forward with the love of your past pet still in your heart.**

Final Thoughts

Legacy projects ensure that **your pet's love continues beyond their lifetime.** Whether through **writing their story, sharing their memory online, or opening your heart to another pet,** their spirit **lives on in the love they left behind.**

Because true love doesn't end—it only finds new ways to grow. 🖤

Final Takeaway for This Chapter

Memorializing your pet is more than just remembering them—it's a way to **honor their love while allowing yourself to heal.** Whether through quiet reflection, creating a tribute, or giving back in their name, these acts of remembrance help **transform grief into something meaningful.**

There is no single "right" way to honor them. **What matters most is choosing what feels true to your heart**—whether it's a personal ritual, a lasting tribute, or carrying their love forward in new ways.

By turning grief into meaningful action, you create **a legacy of love that continues beyond their lifetime.**

Action Step:

Choose **one way to honor your pet's memory** from this chapter and take the **first step toward implementing it this week.** Whether it's lighting a candle, writing their story, or donating in their name, let this act of love **bring you comfort and connection.** ♥

CHAPTER 6

Finding Meaning After Loss— Transforming Grief into Growth

"What if your pet's love didn't end with their passing, but instead became the spark for something greater? What if, instead of just grieving their loss, you used their memory to bring more love, kindness, and purpose into your life?"

Grief has the power to transform us. While losing a beloved pet is heartbreaking, it can also lead to profound personal growth. Many people find that their pet's love continues to shape their lives, inspiring them to become more compassionate, resilient, and open to new experiences. In this chapter, we'll explore how to find meaning in your loss, use your grief as a tool for emotional healing, and allow your pet's memory to guide you toward a more fulfilling future.

Understanding the Role of Grief in Personal Growth: Why Grief Can Be a Catalyst for Change

Grief is often seen as something to endure—a painful chapter we simply have to get through. But in reality, **grief is also a teacher.** It changes us, deepens us, and often leads us to a greater understanding of **ourselves, our emotions, and the meaning of love.**

Losing a pet is heartbreaking, but in the process of mourning, we gain something as well: **a new perspective on life, love, and what truly matters.**

How Loss Deepens Our Emotional Awareness: Grief as a Path to Self-Discovery

When we lose a beloved pet, we're forced to **sit with emotions that run deeper than we may have ever experienced before.** Grief has a way of **cracking us open, revealing parts of ourselves we may not have fully understood.**

💜 **It teaches us about vulnerability.** Losing a pet reminds us that love—true, unconditional love—comes with risk. It shows us that allowing ourselves to love deeply also means we will hurt deeply when that love is lost.

💬 **It expands our emotional depth.** After experiencing profound loss, many people become **more empathetic, more understanding, and more attuned to the emotions of others.**

🔺 **It forces us to process emotions instead of avoiding them.** In daily life, we often push difficult emotions aside. But grief doesn't allow that—it demands to be felt, processed, and honored. **And through that process, we grow.**

This is why grief is often described as a **journey**—because it takes us somewhere new, somewhere deeper within ourselves.

The Paradox of Pain and Love: Profound Grief Exists Because of Profound Love

The intensity of grief can feel unbearable, but **it is only so strong because love was so deep.** The pain of loss is a reflection of the bond we shared, the memories created, and the irreplaceable role our pet played in our lives.

🐾 **Grief is proof of love.** Instead of seeing pain as something negative, we can begin to understand it as **evidence of a love that was real, meaningful, and deeply felt.**

🐾 **Love never disappears—it transforms.** The love you shared with your pet doesn't vanish when they pass. It remains **woven into your heart, your memories, and even the way you live your life moving forward.**

🐾 **We don't grieve what we didn't love.** If the pain is overwhelming, it's because the love was immeasurable. **And that love, even in grief, is something to cherish.**

How Grief Shifts Our Perspective on Life: Appreciating Life's Fragility and Beauty

Grief changes the way we see the world. Losing a pet reminds us of something we often forget in our busy lives: **time is fleeting, love is precious, and the small moments matter most.**

🌿 **We learn to slow down.** After experiencing loss, we often become more mindful of the present—**cherishing the love we have, the connections we share, and the simple joys of everyday life.**

🤍 **We appreciate the little things.** The warmth of the sun on a morning walk, the comfort of a quiet evening, the love of those around us—grief reminds us that **these are the moments that matter.**

👻 **We understand that love is worth it, even when it ends in loss.** Grief teaches us that **the depth of our love makes the pain of loss worthwhile**—and that despite the sorrow, we would choose love again in an instant.

Losing a pet often inspires people to **live with more purpose, love more fully, and appreciate every moment with the people and animals they still have.**

Final Thoughts

Grief is not just about loss—it's about **transformation.** It deepens our emotional awareness, helps us understand the paradox of pain and love, and shifts the way we see the world.

Though painful, grief has the power to make us **more compassionate, more present, and more grateful for the love we have experienced.**

Because in the end, **grief is not just about saying goodbye—it's about honoring the love that will always remain.** ♥

The Science of Post-Traumatic Growth: How Loss Can Lead to Strength and Transformation

Losing a pet can feel like an emotional earthquake—leaving us shaken, vulnerable, and uncertain about how to move forward. But while grief is undeniably painful, research shows that **adversity can also be a catalyst for profound personal growth.**

This process is known as **post-traumatic growth**—the idea that after experiencing deep loss, many people emerge **stronger, more resilient, and with a clearer sense of purpose.**

How Adversity Fosters Personal Transformation: The Science of Growth After Loss

While grief often feels overwhelming, psychological research suggests that **loss can lead to significant personal transformation.** Studies on **post-traumatic growth (PTG)** show that many people, after experiencing profound adversity, report:

💡 **A greater appreciation for life** – Loss can sharpen our awareness of how precious time is, making us more present and intentional in our daily lives.

💜 **Stronger emotional resilience** – After moving through deep grief, people often become more emotionally strong and better able to handle life's challenges.

🌱 **Newfound purpose and meaning** – Many people report that loss shifts their priorities, leading them to **give back, make changes, or embrace life more fully.**

📖 **Scientific Insight:**

Studies on resilience have found that **people who process their grief rather than suppress it are more likely to experience growth after loss.** The process of grieving, when done with self-compassion, allows us to **adapt, reflect, and emerge with a deeper understanding of ourselves and life itself.**

Emotional Resilience Through Loss: Learning to Emerge Stronger

Grief forces us to confront our emotions head-on, which can be **incredibly painful but also incredibly strengthening.** Over time, we begin to recognize that:

💧 **We are capable of surviving deep loss.** At first, grief feels unbearable. But each day we continue to move forward, we realize that we are stronger than we thought.

💜 **Our capacity for love expands.** Losing a pet doesn't diminish our ability to love—it deepens it. Many people find that grief makes them **more compassionate, more** connected, and more appreciative of the relationships they have.

⬤ **We can use our pain to help others.** Some people find that their loss **inspires them to support others going through the same experience.** Whether through advocacy, volunteering, or simply sharing their story, their grief **becomes a source of connection and healing.**

Over time, the sorrow that once felt impossible to bear **shapes us into more resilient, more empathetic versions of ourselves.**

Examples of Pet Owners Who Found Purpose After Loss: Turning Pain Into Action

Many pet owners have transformed their grief into something meaningful—**finding purpose after loss by giving back, creating legacies, and helping others.**

🐾 Lisa's Story: Volunteering to Honor Her Dog

After Lisa lost her Labrador, Toby, she struggled with the silence in her home. Instead of retreating into loneliness, she started **volunteering at a local animal shelter—** walking dogs who had no one else. Over time, she found healing in **helping other animals find the love Toby once had.**

🐾 Mark's Story: Creating a Rescue Fund in Memory of His Cat

Mark's cat, Luna, had been rescued from a difficult situation, and after she passed, he wanted her story to

make a difference. He started a **small fundraiser in her name**, raising money for cat rescues in need. Today, dozens of cats have been saved because of Luna's legacy.

🐾 Emma's Story: Writing to Heal and Inspire Others

When Emma lost her senior dog, Max, she began writing **letters to him in a journal.** Over time, those letters turned into a book about pet loss, helping thousands of grieving pet owners. She found that by **sharing her story, she could help others feel less alone.**

These stories show that **grief doesn't have to be the end of the love we shared—it can be the beginning of something new.**

Final Thoughts

Losing a pet is one of the hardest things we go through, but **grief can also be a gateway to strength, resilience, and renewed purpose.**

Through post-traumatic growth, many people discover:

✔ **A deeper appreciation for life.**

✔ **Emotional resilience they never knew they had.**

✔ **A desire to turn their love into action.**

While the pain of loss is real, so is the **potential for transformation**—because love, when carried forward, has the power to heal not just our hearts, but the lives of others as well. 🖤

Reframing Grief as a Form of Love

Grief can feel like an overwhelming void, an unbearable reminder of what is missing. But at its core, **grief is not just pain—it is love that no longer has a physical place to go.** The bond with your pet doesn't end when they pass; it simply **changes form**.

By shifting our perspective, we can begin to see **grief not as the absence of love, but as proof that love still exists.** And when we embrace this idea, we find healing—not by forgetting, but by **allowing love to continue in new and meaningful ways.**

The Love Never Disappears, Only Changes Form

One of the hardest parts of loss is **feeling like our pet is gone forever**—that their love, their presence, and the connection we shared has vanished. But love isn't something that disappears; **it transforms.**

🐾 **Their love now lives in your heart.** Every memory, every lesson, and every moment you shared is still a part of you.

🐾 **Their presence is still felt in small ways.** Maybe it's a familiar habit they left behind, a scent that lingers, or a quiet moment where you swear you can still sense them nearby.

🐾 **The bond continues, just differently.** Just because you can no longer touch them doesn't mean they aren't still with you—in your thoughts, in your routines, in the ways they shaped who you are.

🐾 A shift in perspective:

Instead of saying *"They are gone,"* try saying *"They are still with me, just in a new way."*

This mindset shift can help transform grief from **a feeling of loss** into **a continued presence of love.**

How Continuing Bonds Theory Helps with Healing

The **Continuing Bonds Theory** suggests that rather than "moving on" from a loved one, we can maintain a **healthy emotional connection** with them. This doesn't mean being stuck in grief—it means finding **gentle ways to carry their love forward.**

🪶 Ways to Maintain a Continuing Bond with Your Pet:

📖 **Speak or write to them** – Whether through journaling or simply talking to them in your thoughts, keeping them in your daily life helps preserve the connection.

🖼 **Keep reminders that bring joy, not pain** – A favorite photo, their collar, or a small keepsake can be a comforting way to feel close to them.

🧘 **Live in a way that honors their spirit** – Whether through kindness, volunteering, or adopting their sense of joy, allowing their love to influence your life is a powerful way to continue the bond.

Instead of viewing grief as **a process of detaching,** this perspective allows us to **integrate their love into our ongoing journey.**

Embracing the Idea That Loss is Not an Ending

One of the most comforting realizations in grief is that **loss does not have to be seen as the end—it can be seen as a transition.**

💡 **Your pet's love continues through you.** Every time you think of them, smile at a memory, or take an action inspired by them, their spirit is alive.

💡 **Their impact remains.** The way they changed you—the joy, patience, or unconditional love they brought into your life—stays with you forever.

💡 **Love is never truly lost.** Instead of focusing on what is gone, consider how their presence continues in ways you may not have expected.

🐾 **Instead of asking, "How do I move on?" try asking, "How do I carry them with me in a way that brings peace?"**

Loss is not the closing of a door—it is the opening of a new way to **experience love.**

Final Thoughts

Grief is **not the opposite of love—it is a continuation of it.** The love you shared with your pet doesn't disappear just because they are physically gone. It **changes, grows, and remains within you in a new form.**

By embracing the idea that loss is not an ending, but **a transformation**, we can begin to heal—not by letting go, but by allowing love to take on a new and beautiful shape. 🖤

Using Your Grief to Create Positive Change: Discovering How Your Pet Changed You

Grief is not just about **what we lost**—it's also about **what we gained** from having loved so deeply. Every pet leaves behind a unique imprint, shaping us in ways we may not even realize.

By reflecting on the lessons they taught us, the ways they helped us grow, and the love they infused into our lives, we can begin to **transform our grief into gratitude and personal growth.**

Reflecting on the Lessons They Taught You

Every pet is a teacher, guiding us in ways both big and small. Even in their absence, the lessons they left behind continue to shape who we are.

🐾 **Patience** – Whether it was house training, waiting for them to stop chasing their tail, or learning to communicate beyond words, our pets **taught us patience and understanding.**

🐾 **Unconditional Love** – They didn't care what we looked like, how much money we made, or whether we had a good or bad day. **Their love was pure, and in receiving it, we learned how to give love more freely.**

❀ **Living in the Moment** – Pets never worry about the future or dwell on the past. They remind us that **joy is found in simple things**—a walk outside, a cozy nap, a shared meal.

❀ **Compassion & Responsibility** – Caring for a pet teaches us what it means to **put another being's needs before our own.** Their dependence on us fosters **empathy, nurturing, and deep commitment.**

Even in their absence, **these lessons remain**—woven into who we are and how we move through the world.

How Their Love Shaped Your Heart

Loving a pet **changes us at our core.** Whether they were with us for a short time or many years, the love we shared **leaves a lasting mark.**

💜 **You became more open-hearted.** Loving a pet teaches us how to be vulnerable, to love without hesitation, and to form deep emotional connections.

💜 **You learned to appreciate the little things.** The wag of a tail, the warmth of a curled-up companion, the quiet comfort of their presence—**they showed you the beauty in everyday moments.**

💜 **You now understand what it means to love selflessly.** Every act of care—feeding them, comforting them when they were sick, making time for them—**was love in action.**

💜 **You carry their love forward.** Even in grief, their love stays within you, influencing how you treat others, how you cherish relationships, and how you continue to love—both humans and animals alike.

Your pet may be gone, but the way they changed you remains.

Journaling Exercises to Explore Your Growth

Writing can be a powerful tool for **self-reflection and healing**. Take time to explore how your pet shaped you by answering the following prompts:

📖 **1. What is one lesson your pet taught you that you still carry today?**

📖 **2. How did your pet's love change the way you love others?**

📖 **3. If you could thank your pet for three things, what would they be?**

📖 **4. What's a habit or routine you developed because of your pet? (And how has it continued?)**

📖 **5. How do you want to carry their memory forward in a way that honors the impact they had on your life?**

Set aside quiet time to reflect, write, and connect with the ways your pet's love still lives within you.

Final Thoughts

Grief is painful, but it is also proof that **our pet's love changed us in beautiful ways.** By reflecting on the lessons they taught us and the ways they shaped our hearts, we can **turn sorrow into gratitude, loss into lasting love.**

Because while they may be gone, **the love they left behind continues to shape the person you are becoming.** 🖤

Finding Purpose Through Your Pain

Grief can feel isolating, but it can also be a bridge—**a way to connect with others, inspire kindness, and express emotions in new and meaningful ways.**

Rather than letting pain consume you, you can **transform it into something that honors your pet's love.** By helping others, engaging in acts of kindness, and channeling your grief into creative expression, you can turn sorrow into **a force for good.**

Helping Others Who Are Grieving: Becoming a Source of Support

No one understands the pain of losing a beloved pet quite like those who have been through it. **By supporting others in grief, you not only help them heal—you also create meaning from your own loss.**

🐾 **Ways to Support Others Who Are Grieving:**

💙 **Listen to someone who is grieving.** Sometimes, just being there and saying *"I understand"* can make all the difference.

📖 **Share your story.** Talking about your pet's life—and your journey through grief—may help someone feel less alone.

💌 **Write a letter of support.** If a friend loses a pet, sending a heartfelt note can provide immense comfort.

⚫ **Join or start a pet loss support group.** Online or in-person groups offer safe spaces for people to share memories and emotions.

Grief, when shared, becomes **a little lighter**. By helping others, you remind them—and yourself—that **love and loss are universal, and no one has to walk this journey alone.**

Engaging in Acts of Kindness in Your Pet's Name

One of the most beautiful ways to **honor your pet's memory** is to **continue their legacy through kindness.**

🐾 **Acts of Kindness Inspired by Your Pet:**

💙 **Leave small notes of encouragement** in public places or online pet loss forums.

🐶 **Donate food or blankets** to a local animal shelter in their name.

🐾 **Pay for a stranger's coffee** or do a random act of kindness, inspired by your pet's unconditional love.

🏠 **Offer to pet-sit for a friend** who needs help.

🤝 **Release a kindness challenge**—encourage others to do something kind in memory of your pet.

Every act of kindness **keeps their spirit alive** and turns grief into something positive—**a ripple of love that extends beyond their time on earth.**

Channeling Grief into Creative Expression

For many, **art is a powerful way to process emotions that words cannot fully express.** Creative expression allows you to **transform grief into something tangible, something beautiful.**

🎨 **Ways to Express Your Grief Creatively:**

📖 **Writing** – Keep a journal, write poetry, or compose letters to your pet. Some even turn their grief into a book that helps others.

🎨 **Painting & Art** – Create a portrait of your pet or an abstract piece that reflects your emotions.

🎵 **Music** – Play a song that reminds you of them, or write a piece in their honor.

📷 **Photography** – Compile a memory book filled with pictures of your pet and the moments you shared.

Creative outlets don't erase grief, but they **help you process it in a way that brings peace.**

Final Thoughts

Pain can either close us off, or it can **open us up to new purpose, deeper love, and meaningful action.**

By supporting others, spreading kindness, and using creative expression to process emotions, you turn grief into a **living tribute**—one that carries your pet's love into the world in a way that never fades. 🖤

Turning Their Legacy into Something Greater

The love your pet gave you was profound, and though their physical presence is gone, their **impact doesn't have to end.** One of the most powerful ways to honor their memory is to **carry their love forward into something that helps others**—whether it's through advocacy, volunteering, or starting a meaningful project in their honor.

By turning your grief into **purposeful action**, you ensure that their legacy **continues to make a difference in the lives of other animals in need.**

Advocating for Animal Welfare: Helping Pets in Need

Losing a beloved pet often deepens our understanding of **how precious and vulnerable animals are.** If their love changed your life, you can honor them by **helping improve the lives of other animals.**

🐾 Ways to Advocate for Animal Welfare in Their Honor:

📣 **Raise awareness about pet adoption** – Share your pet's story to encourage others to adopt instead of shop.

📖 **Educate others about responsible pet care** – Use your experience to help first-time pet owners provide the best care.

✍ **Support animal welfare legislation** – Sign petitions or advocate for laws that protect animals from neglect and cruelty.

💰 **Donate in their memory** – Contribute to shelters, rescue groups, or pet medical funds to help animals in need.

🐶 **Example:** After losing her rescue dog, Bella, Maria began **educating people about the importance of pet adoption**, sharing Bella's story on social media to encourage others to rescue animals in need.

Volunteering at Shelters or Fostering: Finding Healing Through Helping

Helping other animals doesn't mean **replacing your pet**—it means sharing **the love they gave you** with those who need it most.

💜 **Ways to Get Involved:**

🏠 **Foster a pet in need** – Provide temporary love and care for an animal waiting for a forever home.

🐕 **Volunteer at a shelter** – Walk dogs, cuddle cats, or assist with adoption events.

📷 **Use your skills** – If you're a writer, photographer, or social media enthusiast, help shelters spread awareness and find homes for pets.

🎾 **Donate supplies in your pet's name** – Bring toys, food, or blankets to shelters, ensuring other animals feel the comfort your pet once knew.

🐾 **Example:** After her cat, Oliver, passed away, Sophie found comfort in fostering kittens. **Caring for them reminded her of the love she shared with Oliver while giving those in need a second chance.**

Starting a Project in Their Honor: Creating a Legacy That Lasts

If your pet **changed your life**, why not create something that **keeps their memory alive in a meaningful way?**

💡 **Ideas for Legacy Projects:**

🐾 **Create a social media tribute** – Share stories, lessons, and photos that celebrate your pet's life and inspire others.

🏥 **Start a pet medical fund** – Help struggling pet owners afford emergency care.

🐕 **Host an annual event** – A pet-friendly walk, fundraiser, or awareness campaign in their honor.

📖 **Write their story** – Whether it's a blog, a book, or a personal journal, putting their story into words can inspire and comfort others.

🐾 **Example:** When Mark's senior dog, Daisy, passed away, he launched **"Daisy's Blanket Drive,"** collecting blankets every winter for shelter pets. **Her love didn't end with her life—it multiplied.**

Final Thoughts

Your pet's love **changed your life**, and by **turning their legacy into something greater**, you allow that love to **continue making an impact.**

Through advocacy, volunteering, and meaningful projects, you **keep their spirit alive—not just in memory, but in action.**

Because love like theirs **was never meant to end—it was meant to be shared.** 💜

Embracing Life While Keeping Their Spirit Alive: Learning to Love Again Without Guilt

After losing a beloved pet, it can feel impossible to imagine life without them. The grief is deep, the routines feel empty, and the idea of moving forward **can bring feelings of guilt**—as if embracing joy again means leaving them behind.

But **love is not finite**—it doesn't disappear or get replaced. Instead, **it grows, transforms, and finds new ways to express itself.** Moving forward doesn't mean forgetting—it means **allowing the love your pet gave you to continue shaping your life.**

Why Moving Forward Doesn't Mean Forgetting

Many grieving pet owners struggle with guilt at the thought of healing, smiling, or even considering another pet. But it's important to remember:

♡ **Love is not a replacement—it's an expansion.** Welcoming new joy doesn't diminish the love you had; it **adds to the legacy your pet left behind.**

♡ **Healing doesn't erase memories.** The love, lessons, and moments you shared with your pet will **always be a part of you.** Nothing changes that.

♡ **Your pet would want you to be happy.** If they could, they'd nudge you forward with a wag of the tail or a gentle purr—**reminding you that love isn't meant to end in sorrow.**

🐾 **A shift in perspective:** Instead of thinking, *"I'm moving on without them,"* try **"I am moving forward with their love still in my heart."**

Recognizing When You're Ready for New Joy

Grief has no set timeline. Some people feel ready to embrace joy quickly, while others need months or even years. The important thing is to listen to **your own heart**—not outside expectations.

✧ Signs You May Be Ready to Open Your Heart Again:

✔ **You find yourself smiling at memories more than crying over loss.**

✔ **You miss companionship but feel ready to create new memories.**

✔ **Thinking about another pet brings warmth, not just pain.**

✔ **You feel able to give love without feeling like it's a betrayal.**

🐾 **If you're unsure, start small:**

- Spend time around animals—visit a shelter, pet-sit for a friend, or volunteer.

- Picture what life with a new pet would feel like— does the idea bring comfort?

- Remind yourself that love is never "either-or"— **your heart has space for both past and future.**

Letting Your Pet's Memory Guide Your Future Relationships

The love you shared with your pet has shaped you in ways that **don't disappear when they're gone.** Instead, that love can **guide your future relationships—whether with another pet, other people, or even yourself.**

🐾 How Their Love Lives On in Your Future:

🐕 **You'll bring the lessons they taught you into new relationships.** Whether it's patience, gratitude, or simply appreciating the small moments, **your pet's love made you a better person.**

🐾 **You can honor them by continuing to give love.** If they brought you joy, companionship, and comfort, wouldn't they want you to experience that again?

🪶 **You might choose a pet that reminds you of them—or one completely different.** Either choice is okay, as long as it feels right for you.

🐶 **Example:** After losing her dog, Bella, Maria wasn't sure she was ready for another pet. But over time, she realized she missed the routine, the love, and the joy of having a companion. When she adopted a senior dog from a shelter, she felt like she was **paying forward the love Bella had given her—continuing, rather than replacing, the bond.**

Final Thoughts

Loving another pet—or simply allowing joy back into your life—doesn't mean **you are leaving your pet behind.** It means **you are carrying their love forward, letting it continue to shape your life in new and meaningful ways.**

Because love **doesn't end with loss—it finds new ways to grow.** 🖤

Creating a Life They Would Want for You

When grieving a beloved pet, it's natural to wonder, *What would they want for me now?* If they could, **what would they tell you?**

Your pet didn't just love you—they wanted you to be happy. They never worried about the past or the future; they simply lived **each moment with love, joy, and presence.** By embracing the love they gave and carrying it forward, you can **honor their memory by living in a way that reflects the happiness they brought into your life.**

Imagining What They Would Want for You

If your pet could send you a message, it might sound something like this:

🐾 *"I loved our time together, and I want you to be happy—just like you made me happy."*

🐾 *"I don't want you to be stuck in sadness. I want you to find joy again."*

🐾 *"I will always be with you, but you don't have to stop living because I'm gone."*

Rather than holding onto grief as a weight, **let it become a motivation to live a life filled with love, kindness, and presence—because that's what they would want for you.**

Embracing the Love They Gave and Passing It On

Your pet changed your life with their love. **Now, you have the chance to spread that love in new ways.**

🐾 **Ways to Carry Their Love Forward:**

🖤 **Be as kind as they were.** Pets love unconditionally—practice that same kindness toward yourself and others.

🐾 **Help another animal in need.** Whether through adoption, fostering, or simply donating, share the love they gave you with another pet who needs it.

🪶 **Support others going through grief.** Just as you have struggled, someone else will too—offering compassion and understanding can make a world of difference.

🎁 **Do something in their name.** A random act of kindness, a donation to an animal shelter, or a simple moment of love can keep their spirit alive.

👻 **Example:** After losing his dog, Buddy, James made a habit of carrying small dog treats in his pocket. Whenever he met a dog at the park, he'd offer a treat—**a small but meaningful way to continue Buddy's kindness in the world.**

Living With the Same Joy and Curiosity They Had

One of the greatest lessons pets teach us is **how to be present.** They don't dwell on the past or worry about the future—they find joy in the **simple moments.**

🐾 Ways to Honor Their Spirit in Daily Life:

🪦 Find joy in small things – A walk in the park, the warmth of the sun, or a quiet moment of gratitude.

🧸 Be curious and playful – Explore new places, try new things, and don't take life too seriously.

♡ Love fully and without hesitation – Pets never hold back their affection—**let their example remind you to love openly.**

🐕 Example: After her cat, Luna, passed away, Maria decided to live **"more like Luna."** She slowed down, stretched in the morning sunlight, and made an effort to find happiness in the little things—**because that's what Luna would have done.**

Final Thoughts

Your pet wouldn't want you to live in sadness—they would want you to **embrace life with the same love and joy they shared with you.** By living with **kindness, presence, and an open heart,** you honor their memory in the best possible way.

Because the best way to remember them is not just to grieve them, **but to live a life they would be proud of.**
♥

Accepting the Circle of Life

One of the hardest truths of loving a pet is knowing that their time with us is limited. But instead of focusing solely on the pain of loss, we can **honor the beauty of the time we shared, appreciate the larger journey of life, and recognize that love never truly ends.**

Grief may feel like an ending, but in reality, **it is a continuation—a transformation of love into something new.**

Honoring the Beauty of the Time You Shared: Gratitude Over Loss

When faced with loss, it's easy to focus on what was taken from us. But shifting our perspective to **gratitude for the time we had** can ease the pain and allow us to celebrate the love that will always remain.

🐾 **Ways to Focus on Gratitude Instead of Loss:**

💟 **Reflect on the joy they brought.** Every wag of the tail, every purr, every moment of unconditional love was a gift.

📷 **Celebrate their memory with happiness, not just sorrow.** Look through old photos and smile at the beautiful life they lived.

📝 **Make a gratitude list.** Write down the things you're thankful for—**the lessons they taught you, the comfort they gave, and the love you shared.**

🐶 **Example:** Instead of dwelling on the pain of losing her dog, Charlie, Lisa started a daily gratitude practice. **Each morning, she wrote down one happy memory of Charlie.** Over time, this shifted her grief into appreciation.

Seeing Loss as Part of a Larger Journey: The Interconnectedness of Life

In nature, nothing truly ends—**it transforms.** Just as seasons change, love doesn't disappear with loss; **it continues in different forms.**

🌱 **Lessons from Nature:**

- **A sunset marks the end of a day, but it's also the beginning of another.**
- **A fallen leaf nourishes the soil, helping new life grow.**
- **The ocean wave that crashes on shore eventually returns to the sea.**

Your pet was part of a much larger cycle—**one that includes love, loss, transformation, and renewal.** They may be gone in body, but their presence lingers in the ways they changed you, the love they left behind, and the lessons they imprinted on your heart.

🐾 **Example:** When David lost his cat, Willow, he found comfort in nature. He planted a tree in her honor, reminding himself that **life continues, just in a different form.**

Carrying Their Spirit With You Always: Love Never Truly Ends

Though your pet is no longer physically by your side, **their spirit remains with you in the love they left behind.**

🐢 How Their Love Lives On:

💛 **In your habits and routines** – The way you care for others, the patience you learned, and the small things that still remind you of them.

⚫ **In the kindness you share** – Every act of compassion you extend carries their love forward.

🐾 **In the memories that bring you comfort** – They may be gone, but their presence is forever woven into your life.

🐈 **Example:** Every time Sarah saw a golden retriever, she thought of her dog, Bailey. Instead of feeling only sadness, she began to **smile and whisper, "Hi, Bailey," feeling his spirit in those moments.**

The Willow Tree

When Jen lost her cat, Oliver, the silence in her home was deafening. For twelve years, he had been her shadow—curling up beside her as she read, greeting her at the door, and following her from room to room. Without him, the house felt empty, as if something vital had been stripped away.

For weeks, grief clung to her like a heavy fog. She kept expecting to hear the soft thud of his paws jumping onto the windowsill or the quiet purring in the early morning hours. But there was only silence.

One day, while walking through the park where she and Oliver used to sit together, Jen noticed a small sapling growing near the bench. It was a young willow tree, barely knee-high, its fragile branches swaying in the wind. She knelt beside it, running her fingers over the delicate leaves, and something inside her shifted.

She remembered how Oliver used to chase falling leaves in this very spot, pouncing with playful determination. She thought about how, in nature, nothing truly ends— everything transforms. Leaves fall, but they nourish the soil. Flowers wilt, but their seeds grow anew. The love we give never disappears—it simply changes form.

That evening, Jen made a decision. She took a handful of Oliver's ashes and sprinkled them around the base of the willow tree. She wasn't letting go—she was allowing him to become part of something new.

Over the years, the tree grew strong, its branches stretching skyward, providing shade for others who visited the park. Every time Jen passed by, she would pause, lay a hand on its bark, and smile. She no longer looked for Oliver in the empty spaces—she found him in the rustling leaves, the shifting seasons, the quiet presence of something living and growing.

And in that, she understood: he was never truly gone. 🖤

Final Thoughts

Grief is part of the **circle of life**, but so is love. Though loss is painful, it is also **a reminder of how deeply we were blessed to love and be loved.**

By honoring the time you shared, embracing life's interconnected journey, and carrying their spirit with you, **you transform grief into something beautiful—a continued bond that never fades.**

Because love, once given, **never truly leaves.**

Final Takeaway for This Chapter

Grief, while painful, can also be a source of **transformation, growth, and renewed purpose.** It has the power to deepen our understanding of love, strengthen our emotional resilience, and inspire us to live more meaningfully.

Your pet's love **doesn't end with their passing**—it continues in the lessons they taught you, the habits they shaped, and the kindness they brought into your life. By embracing their legacy, you can **carry their spirit forward** in a way that honors the bond you shared.

Finding meaning in loss allows you to **move forward with gratitude, not just sorrow**—knowing that their love **will always be a part of you.**

Action Step:

Write down **three lessons your pet taught you** and **one way you can honor their legacy** by incorporating those lessons into your life moving forward. Whether it's showing more patience, being present in the moment, or sharing kindness with others, let their love **continue to shape your journey.** 🖤

CHAPTER 7

Embracing Healing—Moving Forward Without Leaving Them Behind

"Healing doesn't mean forgetting. It means learning how to carry their love with you in a way that brings peace, not pain."

Many people fear that fully healing from pet loss means "moving on" and leaving their beloved companion behind. But true healing isn't about forgetting—it's about finding a way to live with the love and memories in a way that honors them while allowing yourself to embrace life again. This chapter will help you navigate the final steps of your grief journey, guiding you toward acceptance, peace, and a future where you carry their love with gratitude rather than sorrow.

Redefining What It Means to Move Forward: Letting Go of the Guilt That Comes with Healing

After losing a beloved pet, moving forward can feel impossible—not just because of the pain, but because of

the guilt that sometimes comes with healing. Many pet owners struggle with the fear that **feeling better means forgetting** or that experiencing joy again is a betrayal of the love they shared.

But healing is not about leaving them behind—it's about **carrying their love forward in a way that honors their memory.** By shifting your perspective on grief, you can **release guilt, embrace healing, and redefine what it truly means to move forward.**

Why Grief Can Feel Like a Tether: Understanding the Emotional Attachment to Sadness

Grief isn't just sadness—it's a connection. In the absence of our pet's physical presence, **grief can feel like the only thing we have left of them.** Holding onto sorrow may seem like the only way to **keep them close.**

🐾 **Why We Struggle to Let Go of Grief:**

💔 **Sadness feels like proof of love.** We fear that if we stop grieving, it means our pet wasn't important. But in reality, **love doesn't need pain to exist.**

💔 **Moving forward feels like forgetting.** The thought of no longer crying every day might feel like a sign we're "moving on" without them. But love isn't measured by how long we hurt—it's measured by how deeply we loved.

💔 **Grief becomes part of our identity.** After loss, sadness can feel like a tether to our pet—**but love, not pain, is the real connection.**

Grief is a natural part of the healing process, but **staying in pain forever doesn't mean you loved them more—it just means you haven't allowed yourself to live fully again.**

Reframing Healing as a Tribute to Your Pet: You Honor Them by Living a Happy Life

Instead of thinking of healing as **"moving on,"** consider it a **tribute** to your pet's love. They brought you happiness, comfort, and unconditional love—**wouldn't they want the same for you now?**

🐾 **A New Perspective on Healing:**

🐾 **Your joy is a reflection of the love they gave.** Living a fulfilling life doesn't diminish their importance—it extends their legacy.

♡ **Happiness is not a betrayal—it's a continuation.** The love you shared is not something to be left behind, but something to be **carried forward in new ways.**

🐾 **You honor them by embracing life.** Every moment of peace, kindness, or laughter is a way of saying, *"Thank you for teaching me how to love."*

🐕 **Example:** After losing her dog, Toby, Sarah struggled with guilt over finding happiness again. But she realized that **Toby would never want her to live in sadness.** So, she started taking long walks—something they once loved doing together—as a way to **honor his memory while allowing herself to heal.**

Giving Yourself Permission to Find Joy Again: Recognizing That You Are Not Betraying Their Memory

Healing doesn't mean forgetting. It doesn't mean replacing them or diminishing their importance. **It means choosing to live fully, carrying their love with you.**

💗 **How to Give Yourself Permission to Heal:**

✔ **Acknowledge that grief and joy can coexist.** You can miss them deeply **and still allow yourself to smile.**

✔ **Remember that they would want you to be happy.** If your pet could see you now, would they want you to stay in sorrow—or would they want you to experience love and joy again?

✔ **Take small steps toward joy.** Engage in activities that bring you peace, **without guilt**—whether it's spending time with loved ones, engaging in a hobby, or even opening your heart to another pet when you're ready.

🐾 **Example:** After losing his cat, Luna, Mark felt guilty about enjoying life again. But he realized that every time he laughed, every time he felt peace, he was **honoring the happiness Luna once brought into his life.**

Final Thoughts

Grief doesn't have to be **a weight that keeps you stuck—it can be a bridge to a life that still holds love, joy, and meaning.**

Moving forward **doesn't mean leaving them behind**—it means bringing their love with you in a way that celebrates their life. **By allowing yourself to heal, you are honoring their memory, not betraying it.**

Because the best tribute you can give them is **a life filled with the same love, joy, and warmth they gave you.**

The Balance Between Remembering and Living

Losing a pet is heartbreaking, but their memory doesn't have to be a source of only sadness. **Finding the right balance between remembering and living allows you to cherish their love without feeling trapped in grief.**

Memories should bring comfort, not pain. When grief becomes overwhelming or prevents you from moving forward, it's important to recognize when **a shift is needed**—allowing yourself to heal while still honoring the love they gave you.

Memories as a Source of Comfort, Not Pain

It's natural to miss your pet and feel waves of sadness when remembering them. However, memories should **bring warmth and connection**, not just sorrow. The goal is to **transform grief into gratitude**—so that when you think of them, it's with love and appreciation rather than only loss.

🐾 Ways to Cherish Their Memory Without Pain:

💜 **Smile at the happy moments** – Instead of focusing on the day they left, remember the **years of love they gave.**

📖 **Reframe how you look at old photos** – Let them remind you of the joy they brought instead of only what's missing.

👥 **Celebrate their life, not just mourn their loss** – Find small ways to honor them that bring **peace, not sadness.**

🐶 **Example:** When Emily lost her dog, Bruno, she struggled to look at his pictures. But over time, she started **sharing his funny moments with friends and family.** Eventually, laughter replaced sorrow, and his memory became **a source of comfort instead of pain.**

When Memorials Become Unhealthy: Recognizing When Grief Holds You Back

Memorializing your pet is a beautiful way to honor them—but **when grief prevents you from living, it may be time to reevaluate.** Holding onto their memory should help you heal, not **keep you stuck in sorrow.**

▶ Signs Your Grief May Be Holding You Back:

✗ You feel guilty about experiencing joy or moving forward.

✗ Your home remains unchanged—everything is exactly as it was when they were alive, and it feels painful to adjust.

✗ You avoid certain places, activities, or even conversations because they remind you of your pet.

✗ Your memorial brings **only** sadness, instead of warmth and comfort.

🐾 **What to Do:**

If your pet's memorial is keeping you in a place of **constant grief instead of healing**, consider **making small, gentle changes** to shift your perspective. Adjusting a memorial space, incorporating joyful memories, or finding a new way to honor them **can help create a balance between remembering and living.**

🐕 **Example:** After her cat, Max, passed away, Mia kept his bed untouched for over a year. Every time she saw it, it made her cry. Eventually, she realized that instead of bringing comfort, it was **a painful reminder.** She decided to **turn the space into a small plant corner in his honor**—a tribute that helped her feel **connected, rather than stuck in sadness.**

Creating a Personal Ritual of Release: A Symbolic Way to Accept Healing

Letting go of pain **doesn't mean letting go of love**—it means making space for healing. Creating a **personal ritual of release** can help **symbolize acceptance and growth**, allowing you to move forward with peace.

🪶 Ideas for a Healing Ritual:

✉️ **Write a letter to your pet** – Express everything in your heart, then place it in a memory box or release it in nature.

🕯️ **Light a candle and say a message of gratitude** – Thank them for their love and allow yourself to embrace healing.

🌊 **Release something into nature** – Scatter flowers in a river, plant a tree in their memory, or send a biodegradable lantern into the sky.

🖼️ **Transform their memorial into something joyful** – Adjust their tribute space to **reflect love and gratitude rather than just loss.**

🐾 **Example:** After losing her rabbit, Daisy, Sarah wrote down her favorite memories and buried the note under a new flower in her garden. **Every time she saw it bloom, she felt Daisy's presence in a new and peaceful way.**

Final Thoughts

There is a delicate balance between **honoring the past and embracing the present.** Your pet's memory should be **a source of love and warmth, not something that keeps you from living.**

By transforming grief into gratitude and creating **a symbolic ritual of release**, you allow yourself to **heal while still carrying their love forward.**

Because remembering them should **bring comfort, not pain.** 🖤

Acknowledging That Healing Is Not Linear

Healing from pet loss isn't a straight path—it's a journey filled with ups and downs. **Grief doesn't follow a schedule, and it doesn't end on a specific day.** One moment, you may feel at peace, and the next, a small reminder may bring back a wave of sadness. **That's normal.**

Understanding that grief **comes in waves, managing triggers, and learning to remember without reliving the pain** can help you navigate the healing process with **compassion and patience for yourself.**

Grief Comes in Waves, Not Stages

Many people think of grief as something that happens in stages—**denial, anger, bargaining, depression, and acceptance.** But in reality, **grief is not a checklist—it's a cycle that flows in and out, sometimes when you least expect it.**

🐾 **What to Expect as You Heal:**

🐾 Some days will feel normal, while others might bring fresh pain—**even years later.**

💬 Certain moments will feel joyful, while others might leave you feeling deeply emotional.

♡ Healing isn't about "getting over it"—**it's about learning to carry love and loss together.**

🐾 **Example:** After months of healing, Daniel thought he had finally reached "acceptance" over losing his dog, Jake. But on a random afternoon, he heard a bark that sounded just like Jake's and **was suddenly overwhelmed with emotion.** Instead of feeling like he was "going backward," Daniel reminded himself that grief is a wave—**and waves come and go.**

Healing isn't **a finish line you cross**—it's an evolving process, where love remains and sorrow softens over time.

Triggers and How to Manage Them

Certain moments—special dates, places, or even sounds— **can unexpectedly trigger fresh grief.** These triggers don't mean you're "stuck" in grief; they simply show how deeply you loved.

🐾 **Common Triggers & How to Cope:**

🖼️ **Anniversaries & Special Dates** – Your pet's adoption day, birthday, or the day they passed can be especially emotional. Instead of dreading them, try turning these days into **moments of remembrance**—light a candle, look at photos, or do something they loved.

🐕 **Unexpected Reminders** – A leash hanging by the door, their favorite toy, or seeing a pet that looks like them can bring a sudden wave of grief. When this happens, take a deep breath and **remind yourself that pain is just love with nowhere to go.**

🏠 **Places You Shared Together** – Visiting their favorite park or walking a familiar route can be bittersweet. **When you're ready, revisit these places with love instead of avoidance.**

🐾 **What Helps:**

✔ **Have a coping strategy.** When grief resurfaces, give yourself permission to **pause, reflect, and breathe through it.**

✔ **Turn pain into a moment of honor.** When a trigger appears, say their name, smile at a memory, or whisper *"Thank you for the love you gave me."*

✔ **Give yourself grace.** Feeling sad again doesn't mean you're not healing—it means their love is still a part of you.

🐱 **Example:** When Maya saw another cat sitting in her window—just like her late cat, Whiskers, used to—her eyes filled with tears. Instead of pushing away the emotion, she took a deep breath and **allowed herself to feel gratitude for the years they had together.**

The Difference Between Reliving and Remembering

There's a fine line between **holding onto love** and **holding onto pain.**

🔄 **Reliving**: Replaying the sadness over and over, focusing on regret, guilt, or the pain of their loss.

♡ **Remembering**: Reflecting on their life with warmth, gratitude, and love.

🐾 How to Shift from Reliving to Remembering:

✔ **Focus on their life, not just their loss.** Instead of replaying the last moments, shift your thoughts to the happy ones.

✔ **Speak about them with joy.** Say their name, share stories, and celebrate their impact on your life.

✔ **Let their love inspire your actions.** Honor them by carrying their spirit forward in the way you live and love.

🐶 **Example:** After losing her dog, Max, Lisa found herself constantly reliving his final days. But over time, she made a choice: **instead of only focusing on how he passed, she would focus on how he lived.** She started telling funny Max stories to friends, and each time, she felt a little lighter.

Memories should be a source of comfort, not pain. By shifting the focus from loss to love, **you allow their memory to be a blessing, not a burden.**

Final Thoughts

Healing isn't a straight path—**grief will ebb and flow, but love remains constant.** Triggers may come and go, but they don't erase progress. And remembering **should bring warmth, not just sorrow.**

Give yourself **permission to heal at your own pace**, knowing that moving forward **doesn't mean leaving them behind—it means carrying them with you, always.** 💚

Integrating Their Love into Your Life: Carrying Their Lessons with You

Your pet may no longer be physically by your side, but **their love, their lessons, and their spirit remain a part of you.** Every wag of their tail, every moment of comfort they provided, and every joyful, silly thing they did left an imprint on your heart.

Instead of thinking of grief as something to "move past," consider it something to **integrate—carrying the love they gave you forward into your daily life.**

What Did They Teach You? Reflecting on Their Wisdom

Our pets are some of our greatest teachers. Without words, they show us **what truly matters in life.** When we reflect on their lessons, we realize that their impact goes far beyond their time with us.

🐾 **Lessons Many Pets Teach Us:**

💙 **Patience** – Whether it was waiting for them to learn a new trick or caring for them in old age, they taught you to slow down and love without rushing.

❄ **Joy in Simple Moments** – A patch of sunshine, a good meal, a cozy spot by the window—**they found happiness in the little things, reminding you to do the same.**

🐕 **Unconditional Love** – No matter what kind of day you had, they loved you fully, showing you how to **give and receive love without hesitation.**

🪶 **Presence Over Perfection** – They didn't care about your flaws, your past, or your future. **They lived in the now, and they reminded you to do the same.**

🐾 **Reflection Exercise:** Ask yourself:

- *What was the biggest lesson my pet taught me?*
- *How did their love change the way I see the world?*
- *How can I honor those lessons in my life today?*

Applying Their Wisdom to Your Daily Life

Grief can feel like something that separates us from our pets, but **love is meant to be carried forward.** The best way to honor them is to **live by the lessons they taught you.**

🐾 **Ways to Apply Their Wisdom:**

✔ **Slow down and savor the moment** – Just like they found joy in a warm sunbeam or a gentle scratch behind the ears, take time to **appreciate the small joys in your day.**

✔ **Love openly and without fear** – Just like they loved you without hesitation, choose to show kindness, affection, and gratitude to those around you.

✔ **Prioritize play, rest, and self-care** – Your pet knew how to balance rest and play. **Let them remind**

you that life isn't just about responsibilities—it's about joy, too.

✔ **Forgive quickly and let go of grudges** – They never held onto anger, and they always greeted each day with a fresh start.

🐶 **Example:** After losing her dog, Daisy, Julia realized that Daisy had always been her reason for going on long walks. Instead of stopping the routine, **she kept taking daily walks, using that time to reflect and connect with Daisy's memory.**

Keeping Their Spirit Alive in Your Actions

Your pet's legacy doesn't have to end—it can **live on through you.** Every kind act, every gentle moment of patience, every time you care for another soul, you are **extending the love they gave you into the world.**

🐾 **Ways to Keep Their Spirit Alive:**

💝 **Be kind to animals and people** – Offer love and kindness, just as your pet did every day.

⚫ **Give back in their honor** – Whether it's donating to a shelter, fostering a pet, or simply helping someone in need, **let their love inspire action.**

🎗 **Create a tradition inspired by them** – Light a candle, take a mindful walk, or do something they loved as a way to honor their memory.

🐾 **Use their lessons to shape your choices** – Whether it's choosing patience, embracing joy, or offering unconditional love, **let their memory guide you.**

🐈 **Example:** After losing her cat, Oliver, Mia realized that he always found the coziest spots to nap in the house. Inspired by his love of comfort, she started creating **small self-care rituals—cozy reading time, warm blankets, and quiet moments of peace—allowing his love to continue shaping her life.**

Final Thoughts

Your pet may be gone, but **their love, their lessons, and their spirit live on in you.** By reflecting on what they taught you, applying their wisdom to your daily life, and keeping their memory alive in your actions, you create **a living tribute to their love.**

Because the best way to honor them isn't just to remember them—it's to **let their love continue to shape the way you live.** ❤️

Finding New Sources of Joy Without Replacing Them

After losing a beloved pet, it can feel impossible to imagine joy without them. The routines you shared, the comfort they provided, and the happiness they brought **left a space in your heart that no one else can fill.** But healing isn't about forgetting or replacing them—it's about **allowing your heart to expand, making room for new experiences while still carrying their love with you.**

Recognizing When You're Ready to Open Your Heart Again

Healing doesn't have a timeline. Some people feel ready to welcome joy back into their lives quickly, while others take months or even years. The important thing is to **listen to yourself** and recognize when you're **open to happiness again, without guilt or hesitation.**

🐾 **Signs You May Be Ready for New Joy:**

✔ **Memories bring more warmth than pain.** You still miss them, but thinking of them makes you smile more than cry.

✔ **You feel drawn to companionship.** Whether it's connecting with people, animals, or nature, you find yourself seeking comfort again.

✔ **You want to engage in life again.** Activities that once felt dull or empty start to bring curiosity and interest.

✔ **The idea of love doesn't feel like betrayal.** You understand that welcoming joy doesn't erase the love you had—it honors it.

👻 **Example:** After losing her dog, Bella, Emily initially felt like she could never have another pet. But as time passed, she realized she missed the companionship, the love, and the laughter. She knew she wasn't "replacing" Bella—she was simply **allowing her heart to love again.**

Exploring New Activities That Bring Happiness

Grief often makes everything feel heavy, but **engaging in meaningful activities can help bring light back into your life.** These activities don't have to be about replacing your pet—they can be about **rediscovering what makes life fulfilling.**

🐾 **Ways to Find New Sources of Joy:**

🌿 **Spending time in nature** – Walks, hikes, or simply sitting outside can bring calm and clarity.

📖 **Exploring creative outlets** – Writing, painting, or making music can help process emotions and bring a sense of fulfillment.

♥ **Trying new experiences** – Visiting new places, taking up a hobby, or even volunteering can add fresh meaning to life.

🐕 **Connecting with animals in new ways** – Volunteering at a shelter, fostering, or simply spending time around pets can be comforting.

🐾 **What Matters Most:**

The goal isn't to "move on"—**it's to re-engage with life in a way that feels right to you.** Your pet wouldn't want you to stay stuck in sadness—they would want you to **keep living, keep loving, and keep finding joy.**

🐱 **Example:** After losing her cat, Whiskers, Sarah found that gardening helped bring her peace. Planting flowers and watching them grow became **a quiet way to nurture life, just as she had once cared for Whiskers.**

Understanding That Healing Is About Expansion, Not Replacement

One of the biggest fears after pet loss is that **welcoming new happiness means "replacing" them.** But love doesn't work that way. **Love expands—it doesn't replace.**

♡ **Your pet's love remains with you, always.** Even if you find joy in new ways, their memory will never fade.

♡ **Healing isn't about filling an empty space—it's about growing around it.** Your pet was unique, and nothing can ever take their place, but **your heart has room to love in new ways, too.**

♡ **Choosing joy honors their love.** If they could tell you anything, they'd likely say, *"Be happy, just like you made me happy."*

🐾 **Example:** When David lost his senior dog, Rusty, he thought he could never have another pet. But over time, he realized that **Rusty had taught him how to love selflessly.** When he finally adopted another rescue dog, he felt like **he was continuing Rusty's legacy, not replacing him.**

Final Thoughts

Healing doesn't mean forgetting. **It means expanding— allowing yourself to find new sources of joy while still holding onto the love your pet gave you.**

You're not leaving them behind. **You're carrying them with you, into every new moment of happiness you allow yourself to experience.** ♥

Knowing When (or If) You're Ready for Another Pet

After losing a beloved pet, the thought of bringing another into your life can be both comforting and overwhelming. Some people feel ready right away, while others take months or even years. **There is no right or wrong timeline—only what feels right for you.**

The key is to make sure you are **honoring your past pet's love, not trying to replace it.** A new pet will never be a "substitute," but they can become **a new and unique source of companionship, love, and joy.**

Questions to Ask Yourself Before Making the Decision

Before welcoming another pet, take time to reflect on **whether you're truly ready, emotionally and practically.**

🐾 **Ask Yourself:**

♥ **Am I considering a new pet because I have love to give, not just because I feel lonely?**

♥ **Does thinking about a new pet bring excitement, rather than just sadness or guilt?**

♡ **Am I ready for the responsibility of pet ownership again, with a full heart?**

♡ **Do I understand that this pet will have their own personality and shouldn't be compared to my past pet?**

♡ **Am I making this decision out of love, not out of pressure from others?**

If your answers lean toward **love, excitement, and readiness**, it may be time to **open your heart again.** If you still feel hesitant, that's okay too—**take your time.**

👻 **Example:** After losing his dog, Max, Tom thought about adopting another, but he realized he wasn't quite ready. Instead of rushing, he started volunteering at a shelter, which helped him **heal at his own pace until he felt truly ready.**

Choosing a Pet for the Right Reasons

A new pet will **never replace** the one you lost. Instead, they will bring **their own love, personality, and special moments into your life.**

🐾 **Make Sure You Are Adopting for the Right Reasons:**

✔ **Right Reason:** *"I have love to give, and I want to share my life with another animal."*

✗ **Wrong Reason:** *"I need to fill the emptiness as quickly as possible."*

✔ **Right Reason:** *"I am excited to build a new bond with a pet who is completely unique."*

✗ **Wrong Reason:** *"I want a pet just like the one I lost."*

Every pet deserves to be loved for who they are, not as a replacement for another. Entering this new chapter with **an open heart** allows you to build **a fresh, loving connection.**

🐩 **Example:** When Lisa lost her cat, Shadow, she hesitated to adopt another. She knew no cat could ever be the same. But one day, she met a rescue kitten who **had completely different traits but still made her heart feel full again.**

How to Introduce a New Pet While Keeping Your Past Companion's Memory Alive

Welcoming a new pet doesn't mean **forgetting the one who came before.** You can still **honor their memory while embracing new beginnings.**

🐾 **Ways to Keep Their Spirit Alive While Bonding with a New Pet:**

📖 **Create a tribute space** – Keep a framed photo, a special keepsake, or plant a tree in their honor.

💬 **Speak about them openly** – Saying their name, sharing stories, and remembering them with love keeps their spirit close.

🐶 **Adopt a tradition they loved** – If your past pet loved morning walks or cuddling before bed, keep those small rituals alive.

🐾 **Let your new pet be themselves** – Avoid comparisons and embrace their unique quirks and personality.

🐾 **Example:** When Jason adopted a new puppy after losing his senior dog, he kept a **small paw print charm on his keychain as a way to carry both dogs with him.** He loved his new pet **without feeling like he had to "replace" his old one.**

Final Thoughts

Bringing a new pet into your life **isn't about moving on—it's about moving forward, with love.**

When the time feels right, and your heart is open, a new pet can become **a fresh, beautiful chapter—one that doesn't erase the past but continues the journey of love.**

Because love **never runs out—it only grows.**

Creating a Life That Honors Their Memory: Turning Grief Into Gratitude

Grief is often seen as something we must endure, but **what if we could transform it into something beautiful?** Instead of focusing on what was lost, we can shift our perspective to **appreciate what was gained—the love,** the lessons, and the irreplaceable moments we shared.

By embracing gratitude, we don't erase our pain, but we allow love to take center stage. **Grief softens when we replace sorrow with appreciation, turning our pet's memory into a source of comfort rather than just loss.**

Shifting from Loss to Appreciation: Focusing on the Love They Brought

Losing a pet is heartbreaking, but **grief exists because love existed first.** Instead of focusing on the pain of their absence, we can remind ourselves:

🐾 **What if, instead of grieving their loss, we celebrated their love?**

🐾 **What if, instead of mourning their departure, we cherished every moment they were here?**

🐾 **What if, instead of focusing on the end, we honored the beautiful life they lived?**

Shifting to gratitude doesn't mean **ignoring sadness—it means letting love outweigh the pain.**

♡ **Instead of saying, "I lost them," try thinking, "I was lucky to have them."**

♡ **Instead of thinking, "They're gone," remind yourself, "Their love is still with me."**

♡ **Instead of dwelling on what you miss, focus on what you were given.**

🐶 **Example:** After losing her dog, Charlie, Mia realized she had spent weeks only thinking about his last day. One afternoon, she sat down and listed **all the things she loved about him—the way he ran in circles when excited, the way he rested his head on her lap.** For the first time since his passing, she smiled through the tears.

Keeping a Gratitude Journal in Their Honor: Writing Down the Joy They Gave You

One of the most powerful ways to **shift from grief to gratitude** is through journaling. Writing helps process emotions, and a **gratitude journal dedicated to your pet** can become a way to **keep their love present in your life.**

📖 **How to Start a Pet Gratitude Journal:**

♡ **Write a memory a day.** A funny moment, a time they comforted you, a lesson they taught you.

🐾 **List the ways they changed your life.** How did they make you a better person?

❋ **Write letters to them.** Tell them how much they meant to you and what you're doing to honor them.

🐕 **Include photos, drawings, or small mementos.** Anything that makes you feel connected to them.

A gratitude journal **doesn't erase the pain, but it transforms grief into something meaningful.** It turns memories into treasures, letting their love **remain active in your life.**

🐾 **Example:** Every night before bed, Adam wrote down one happy memory of his late cat, Luna. Over time, these memories **became a source of comfort,** allowing him to feel close to her without overwhelming sadness.

Celebrating the Life You Had Together Instead of Mourning the Loss

Your pet's life was **so much more than the day they passed.** Instead of letting grief define their story, choose to celebrate **the joy they brought into the world.**

🐾 **Ways to Celebrate Their Life:**

🎉 **Tell their story.** Share funny or heartwarming memories with friends, family, or on social media.

🌿 **Do something in their honor.** Donate to an animal rescue, volunteer, or start a tradition inspired by them.

📷 **Make a photo album or scrapbook.** Fill it with your favorite pictures and notes about their quirks and personality.

🏛 **Have a celebration day.** Instead of focusing on the day they passed, choose a day each year to celebrate the love they gave you.

🐶 **Example:** Instead of dreading the anniversary of his dog, Buddy's, passing, Ryan decided to **make it a day of celebration.** Each year, he donates toys to a local shelter and takes a long walk—just as he and Buddy always did. **Now, the day brings warmth instead of only pain.**

Final Thoughts

Grief and gratitude **can coexist.** You can miss your pet and still feel lucky to have had them. You can feel pain but still **choose to focus on love.**

By keeping a **gratitude journal, sharing their story, and celebrating the time you had together,** you ensure that their memory remains a **source of warmth, not just sorrow.**

Because their love **was a gift—and that's something to be grateful for.** 🖤

Giving Back in Their Name

One of the most beautiful ways to honor your pet's memory is to **carry their love forward**—turning grief into action and keeping their spirit alive through kindness. Whether through **small everyday gestures or larger commitments**, giving back allows you to transform sorrow into **a lasting legacy of love.**

By helping other animals, supporting those who are grieving, or spreading the joy your pet brought into your life, you ensure that **their impact continues far beyond their time with you.**

Ways to Continue Their Legacy: Small or Big Actions That Spread Their Love

Honoring your pet doesn't have to be complicated—**small acts of love can make a big impact.** Every gesture that reflects the kindness they brought into your life is a way to keep their spirit alive.

🐾 Simple Ways to Continue Their Legacy:

💜 **Random acts of kindness in their name** – Pay for someone's coffee, leave a kind note, or donate pet food to a shelter.

🐕 **Keep their traditions alive** – If they loved long walks, take one in their honor; if they adored treats, bake some for a friend's pet.

🌸 **Plant a tree or flowers in their memory** – A living tribute that grows just as their love did.

📷 **Create a photo book or video montage** – Share their story with friends and family so their spirit remains part of your life.

🐶 **Example:** After losing her dog, Molly, Sarah started **leaving small dog treats at her neighborhood park with a note: "A gift from Molly, who loved this park."** Each time she visited, she saw other dogs enjoying the treats, and it made her feel like **Molly's love was still being shared.**

Helping Other Animals as a Way to Heal

Many pet owners find **comfort and healing** by helping other animals in need. **Your pet gave you so much love—imagine passing that love on to another animal who needs it.**

🐾 Ways to Help Other Animals:

🏠 **Foster a pet in need** – If you're ready, fostering can be a temporary but deeply rewarding way to give an animal love.

🐕 **Volunteer at a shelter or rescue** – Walk dogs, socialize cats, or assist with adoption events in honor of your pet.

🎁 **Donate supplies in their name** – Many shelters need food, blankets, and toys—**giving in your pet's honor ensures their love continues to help others.**

🦴 **Sponsor a rescue animal** – Many organizations allow you to sponsor medical care, food, or shelter for a pet in need.

🐾 **Example:** When David lost his cat, Luna, he wasn't ready for another pet. Instead, he started **volunteering at a cat rescue, comforting shy cats who needed human interaction.** He found that giving love to other animals helped **heal his heart while continuing Luna's legacy.**

Sharing Your Story to Help Others Experiencing Pet Loss

One of the hardest parts of losing a pet is feeling **alone in your grief.** But sharing your story can **help others who are struggling,** letting them know that **they are not alone.**

🐾 Ways to Support Others Through Your Story:

📝 **Write about your journey** – Whether through social media, a blog, or a journal, sharing your experience can bring comfort to those grieving.

💬 **Offer support in pet loss groups** – Online and in-person pet loss communities provide a safe space to share stories and healing advice.

🎗 **Create a memorial project** – A Facebook page, a tribute video, or a special event in your pet's name can inspire others to celebrate their own pets.

🐶 **Be there for a friend who is grieving** – If you know someone who recently lost a pet, offer **kindness, empathy, and understanding—just as you wish someone had done for you.**

🐾 **Example:** After losing her beloved dog, Rocky, Maria started **a small online support group** for grieving pet owners. It became a place where people could **share memories, offer encouragement, and find healing through community.**

Final Thoughts

Giving back in your pet's name **ensures that their love continues to touch lives, even beyond their time here.** Whether through **helping other animals, supporting grieving pet owners, or spreading kindness in their memory**, you are keeping **their spirit alive in the most meaningful way.**

Because their love **was never meant to end—it was meant to grow.** 🖤

Living with an Open Heart

Losing a beloved pet can make it feel as though a piece of your heart is missing. The love you shared was deep, unconditional, and unlike any other relationship. But while grief can make us hesitant to open our hearts again, **choosing to love once more doesn't diminish what you lost—it honors it.**

Love, once given, never fades. It continues **in the way we live, in the kindness we share, and in the bonds we form moving forward.**

Allowing Yourself to Love Deeply Again

Grief can sometimes make us fearful of forming new bonds. The pain of loss may whisper that it's easier to **protect yourself from future heartbreak** rather than risk loving again. But love is **not meant to be guarded— it's meant to be given freely.**

🐾 **Why It's Okay to Love Again:**

🖤 **Your heart doesn't have a limit on love.** Just as having one friend doesn't mean you can't have another, loving a new pet or person **doesn't take away from the love you had before.**

🖤 **Choosing love is a tribute to what you lost.** The best way to honor your pet's love is to continue **living with the same open heart they inspired in you.**

♡ **Love isn't about replacing—it's about expanding.** Welcoming love again doesn't erase their memory; it **carries their spirit forward into your next chapter.**

🐶 **Example:** When Emily lost her cat, Whiskers, she thought she could never open her heart again. But over time, she realized that **Whiskers had taught her how to love deeply.** When she finally adopted another cat, she saw it not as replacing Whiskers, but as **continuing the love Whiskers had brought into her life.**

Using Their Love to Enhance Your Life

The love you shared with your pet **didn't end—it became a part of you.** Whether it was patience, joy, or the ability to find happiness in small moments, their love **shaped who you are today.**

🐾 **Ways to Carry Their Love Into Your Future:**

🪶 **Live with presence.** Just like your pet cherished each moment, remind yourself to **appreciate the now.**

🐾 **Show unconditional kindness.** Offer love and patience to those around you, just as your pet did for you.

🐾 **Keep their memory alive in your actions.** Whether it's volunteering, fostering, or simply sharing their story, let **their love inspire how you give to the world.**

🐕 **Example:** After losing his dog, Buddy, James found himself more patient and compassionate—not just with animals, but with people. **He realized that Buddy had**

made him a better person, and he carried that lesson into everything he did.

Understanding That Love, Once Given, Never Fades

Love is not bound by time, space, or loss. The love you shared with your pet **remains in your heart, in the memories you cherish, and in the way you continue to love.**

♡ **Your pet's love lives on:**

✔ **In the lessons they taught you.** Every act of kindness, patience, and joy is a reflection of them.

✔ **In the way you treat others.** The warmth and love they gave you can now be shared with the world.

✔ **In the memories that make you smile.** Their love is forever woven into your life's story.

🐾 **Example:** Every morning, Maria still whispers, "Good morning, Max," even though her dog is no longer physically there. It's a small, quiet reminder that **his love is still with her, always.**

A New Chapter of Love

When Mark lost his Labrador, Bella, the silence in his home was unbearable. For twelve years, Bella had been his shadow—following him from room to room, curling up at his feet, and greeting him every morning with a wagging tail. Without her, everything felt empty.

For months, he told himself he wasn't ready for another dog. No one could replace Bella. He kept her leash by the door, her favorite blanket folded neatly on the couch, and her water bowl untouched in the corner. Every time he thought about getting another pet, guilt crept in.

"If I bring home another dog, will it mean I'm forgetting her?"

One day, while running errands, Mark passed by an animal shelter. He hadn't planned to stop, but something pulled him inside. As he walked through the rows of kennels, he felt his chest tighten—so many dogs, all waiting for love.

Then he saw Bailey.

A young rescue dog with big brown eyes and a cautious tail wag, Bailey was nothing like Bella. He was smaller, wiry, and had a nervous energy about him. But when Mark knelt down, Bailey inched forward, pressing his forehead against Mark's hand, as if he'd been waiting for this moment.

Mark felt his heart soften. He wasn't replacing Bella—he was making space for new love.

Bringing Bailey home wasn't easy. He was shy, hesitant, unsure. He didn't know how to trust, and at first, neither did Mark. But each day, they found comfort in each other— Bailey learning that he was safe, and Mark realizing that love doesn't replace love; it only expands.

One evening, as Bailey curled up beside him, Mark reached for Bella's old blanket and draped it over them both. Bella's love hadn't disappeared. It had simply made room for something new.

And in that moment, he knew: Bella would have wanted this. 🖤

Final Thoughts

Living with an open heart **doesn't mean forgetting—it means carrying love forward.**

The bond you shared with your pet is eternal, and it continues in the **way you live, the way you love, and the kindness you bring into the world.**

Because love, once given, **never truly leaves—it simply finds new ways to shine.** 🖤

Final Takeaway for This Chapter

Healing isn't about letting go—it's about **learning to live with love instead of loss.** Your pet's memory isn't something you have to leave behind; it's something you carry with you, woven into your heart forever. No matter how much time passes, **the love they gave you will always be a part of who you are.**

Moving forward doesn't mean forgetting. It means embracing life with the same **joy, love, and kindness** they brought into yours. **Choosing to love again, whether through new experiences, relationships, or even another pet, is not a betrayal—it's a tribute.** It's a continuation of the love they gifted you, spreading it further into the world.

The best way to honor them is to **live with an open heart, just as they did—fully, freely, and without fear.**

Action Step:

Write a letter to your pet expressing gratitude for everything they brought into your life. **Tell them what they meant to you, what you miss, and how you will carry their love forward.** Let this be a promise—**to live in a way that keeps their memory alive, not in sadness, but in love.** ♥

A Journey of Love, Loss, and Lasting Connection

"Grief is not a sign of weakness, nor is healing a sign of forgetting. Both are proof of the love you shared—and the love that will always remain."

Losing a pet is one of the most painful experiences a person can endure, but it is also a testament to the deep love and bond you shared. If you've made it this far in the book, you've taken courageous steps toward healing, understanding your grief, and finding ways to honor your beloved companion.

This is not the end of your journey. It is a turning point— one where grief no longer holds you captive, but instead, love and gratitude lead the way.

Reflecting on Your Healing Journey: Recognizing How Far You've Come

Grief can feel like an endless road when you're in the middle of it, but when you pause and look back, you'll see that **you've come so much farther than you once thought possible.** Healing is not about forgetting; it's about **learning to carry love differently, allowing your heart to hold both sorrow and joy.**

Now is the time to recognize the **strength within you—** to acknowledge the progress you've made, the love that still exists, and the ways you have honored your pet's memory. **Even if grief still lingers, you are not in the same place where you began.**

Look Back at Where You Started: Acknowledging the Raw Pain

In the beginning, the loss felt unbearable. The quiet spaces in your home, the empty routines, the aching absence of their presence—**it all felt too much to bear.** You may have questioned if you would ever feel whole again, if the grief would ever loosen its grip on your heart.

💜 **Remember those early days:**

- The tears that fell easily.

- The longing for just one more moment with them.

- The way everything reminded you of them—how it hurt just to look at their favorite spot.

That pain was real, and it was valid. But even in the depth of sorrow, **you kept going.** Even on the hardest days, you faced the grief instead of running from it. **You survived those first, impossible moments.** And that alone is worth recognizing.

🙂 **Example:** When Emily lost her cat, Jasper, she couldn't walk into the living room without feeling overwhelmed by his absence. She avoided it for weeks. But slowly, she started sitting there again, placing a small photo of him on the table as a reminder that his presence, while changed, was still with her.

See the Progress You've Made: Recognizing Small but Meaningful Steps

Grief doesn't heal in an instant—it heals **through small, quiet steps forward.** You may not have noticed them at the time, but every little moment of resilience has been part of your healing.

🐾 **Signs of Your Progress:**

🪶 **You can talk about your pet with more love than pain.**

🤍 **Memories bring smiles along with tears.**

🐾 **You have found new ways to honor their memory—rituals, traditions, or simple moments of reflection.**

🔒 **You have allowed yourself to experience joy again, even if it felt impossible in the beginning.**

Each small step was **a victory**—proof that love is stronger than grief and that healing is happening, even when it doesn't feel like it.

🐾 **Example:** After losing her dog, Max, Sarah couldn't bear to go on walks alone. But one day, she went to their favorite trail, not to replace the past, but to remember him in a way that felt peaceful. **It was a small but meaningful step toward healing.**

Celebrate the Strength You've Gained: You Have Endured, You Have Loved, and You Are Healing

The fact that you are here now, reading this, reflecting on your journey, means that **you have faced one of life's greatest heartbreaks and continued forward with love in your heart.** That takes courage. That takes strength.

💜 **You have endured.** The love you shared with your pet was deep, and so was the pain of losing them—but you carried on.

💜 **You have honored their memory.** Whether through storytelling, rituals, giving back, or simply holding them in your heart, **you have kept their love alive.**

💜 **You are healing.** Maybe not perfectly, maybe not completely, but **you are learning how to live again while still carrying their love with you.**

Healing doesn't mean there won't be sad moments ahead, but it does mean that **you have learned how to hold love and loss together—and that is a gift.**

🐶 **Example:** Mark never thought he'd feel whole again after losing his senior dog, Bella. But as time passed, he realized he was still shaped by the love she gave him. He started waking up each morning, whispering, *"Good morning, Bella,"* as a way to keep her presence in his life. **He hadn't let go—he had found a new way to carry her love.**

Final Thoughts

Reflecting on your journey, **you should be proud of yourself.**

You have faced loss and allowed yourself to feel deeply. You have taken steps, no matter how small, toward healing. **You have honored the love you shared with your pet by continuing to live with an open heart.**

As you move forward, carry this truth with you: **Grief may have changed you, but love has shaped you. And love will always remain.** 🖤

The Love You Shared Will Always Be With You

Losing a pet can feel like an unbearable separation, but the truth is, **love doesn't end—it transforms.** Even though they are no longer physically beside you, **their presence remains in your heart, in your memories, and in the way they shaped your life.**

You may no longer hear the sound of their paws on the floor, feel their warm presence curled beside you, or see their excited greeting when you walk through the door. But in many ways, **they are still with you—woven into your daily life, your habits, and your heart.**

Love is not something that disappears. **It remains, just in a different form.**

Love Doesn't End, It Transforms

The bond you shared with your pet was real, deep, and unbreakable. Their love doesn't vanish with their passing; it simply **changes into something new—something just as powerful, just as present.**

🐾 **How Their Love Continues in Your Life:**

♡ **In the routines you keep** – Maybe you still take evening walks or wake up expecting them beside you. Their presence lingers in the small habits they left behind.

🪶 **In the moments they send you signs** – A familiar sound, a sudden warm memory, a dream where they visit you—little reminders that their spirit is still near.

🐕 **In the way you love others** – The patience, kindness, and unconditional love they gave you is now part of how you care for the people and animals in your life.

🐾 **Example:** After losing her cat, Luna, Rachel sometimes still felt her jumping onto the bed, even though she was gone. Instead of feeling sad, she smiled and whispered, *"I know you're still with me."*

Your pet's love **isn't lost—it simply takes a new form, one that will remain with you always.**

How Their Memory Continues to Shape You

Your pet wasn't just a companion; **they were a teacher, a source of comfort, and a constant presence in your life.** They shaped the way you love, the way you see the world, and even the way you carry yourself today.

🐾 **Ways Their Memory Continues to Influence You:**

❇️ **The lessons they taught you live on** – Maybe they taught you patience, how to live in the moment, or how to appreciate the little things.

💜 **Their joy left a mark on your heart** – Whether it was their playful energy, their soothing presence, or their unconditional love, **their happiness became part of you.**

🐶 **You carry their love forward** – In the way you treat animals, in the kindness you show others, and in the way you care for yourself.

🐾 **Example:** After losing her dog, Charlie, Emma realized that he had taught her how to appreciate the simple joys—**a walk in the fresh air, a cozy nap, a moment of quiet contentment.** Now, even without him, she carried those lessons into her daily life.

They shaped you, and that part of them will never fade.

You Are Forever Changed by Their Love

You are not the same person you were before they came into your life—and you are not the same person you were before they left. **Their love has left an imprint on your soul, one that time will never erase.**

💜 **You are more compassionate because of them.**

💜 **You understand unconditional love because of them.**

💜 **You have learned to cherish the present because of them.**

Their time with you may have been shorter than you wished, but **their impact on your heart is permanent.**

🐾 **Example:** Every time Daniel saw a golden retriever, he thought of his dog, Buddy. Instead of feeling pain, he felt gratitude—**because Buddy had shaped his heart, and that love would always be part of him.**

Final Thoughts

Your pet's love **is not something you have to let go of.** It is something that lives within you, shapes you, and walks beside you in a new way. **They may not be physically here, but their love will always be a part of you.**

Because love doesn't disappear. **It stays. It transforms. It remains forever.** 💜

What You've Learned About Yourself

Grief has a way of revealing **who we truly are**—our capacity to love deeply, to endure loss, and to find our way forward even in the hardest moments. Through the pain of losing your pet, you have learned that **grief is not just about saying goodbye—it is about learning how to carry love in a new way.**

This journey has taught you about your own resilience, strength, and the ability of your heart to **heal while still holding on to love.** You may not have chosen this path, but **you have walked it with courage, and that is worth recognizing.**

Grief is a Journey, Not a Destination

When you first lost your pet, it may have felt like **grief was something you needed to "get through"—a mountain to climb, an obstacle to overcome.** But over time, you've learned that **grief doesn't work that way.**

💗 **There is no finish line—only a continued path.** Some days will feel lighter, some will feel heavy, and that's okay.

💗 **Healing isn't about forgetting—it's about learning to live with love instead of loss.**

💗 **Grief may change over time, but love remains constant.**

You are not the same person you were at the beginning of this journey. You have learned that **grief doesn't disappear, but it becomes easier to carry.** The love you shared with your pet continues, not in sorrow, but in memory, gratitude, and quiet moments of reflection.

🐾 **Example:** In the early days after losing her cat, Milo, Sarah believed she had to "move on" from the pain. But over time, she realized that **grief wasn't something to get over—it was something to walk with.** She allowed herself to remember Milo with love, not just sadness, and that made all the difference.

You Are More Resilient Than You Thought

There were moments when the grief felt unbearable—when you questioned how you could move forward without them. And yet, **here you are.** Still standing, still loving, still honoring their memory. **You have survived the hardest days, and that is proof of your strength.**

🐾 **How This Journey Has Shown Your Resilience:**

💜 **You faced loss head-on.** Even when it hurt, you didn't run from your emotions—you allowed yourself to feel, to grieve, and to heal.

🦴 **You kept moving forward, even in small ways.** Whether it was talking about them, creating a memorial, or simply getting through a hard day, you continued to live.

🐕 **You honored their love instead of being consumed by loss.** Instead of letting grief define you, you've chosen to **let love be what remains.**

You are stronger than you ever realized. **Your heart didn't break beyond repair—it adapted, it endured, and it found ways to carry love forward.**

🐾 **Example:** After losing his dog, Max, James thought he would never feel joy again. But little by little, he found himself smiling at memories, taking long walks in Max's honor, and even comforting others who had lost their pets. **He had discovered a strength he never knew he had.**

Your Heart Has the Capacity to Heal and Love Again

Losing a pet can make it feel as though your heart will never be whole again. But through this journey, you have learned that **healing doesn't mean forgetting—it means making space for love to continue.**

🐾 **What You've Discovered About Your Heart:**

💙 **Pain and love can coexist.** You can miss your pet and still find joy in life.

💙 **Healing is possible.** The ache may never fully go away, but it will soften, allowing love to take its place.

💙 **Your heart is still capable of love.** Whether it's through deepening relationships, embracing new experiences, or even welcoming another pet when you're ready, **your ability to love is still strong.**

Your pet's love didn't just disappear when they passed. **It lives within you, shaping how you move forward, reminding you that love, once given, never fades.**

🐾 **Example:** At first, Laura couldn't imagine loving another pet after losing her beloved dog, Daisy. But over time, she realized that **Daisy had taught her how to love fearlessly and completely.** When she eventually adopted another rescue, she did so not to replace Daisy, but to **continue the love Daisy had given her.**

Final Thoughts

This journey has been one of love, loss, and transformation. Through it all, **you have learned that grief is not a road with an endpoint, but a path that continues.**

You have discovered your resilience, your ability to carry love forward, and the truth that **healing is possible— not by letting go, but by holding on in a different way.**

Because love doesn't disappear. **It grows, it changes, and it remains—forever.** 🖤

Carrying Their Legacy Forward: Honoring Your Pet in Your Everyday Life

Your pet may no longer be physically beside you, but their love, their lessons, and their presence **are still part of you.** Every wag of their tail, every comforting purr, every joyful moment you shared has left an imprint on your heart.

Carrying their legacy forward isn't about **holding onto grief—it's about holding onto love.** It's about **living in a way that reflects the kindness, joy, and unconditional love they brought into your life.**

Living in a Way That Reflects Their Love

Your pet loved without hesitation, forgave without conditions, and found joy in the simplest moments. **What** better way to honor them than by carrying those qualities into your own life?

🐾 **Ways to Reflect Their Love in Your Daily Life:**

🖤 **Practice kindness** – Whether to animals or people, extend the same love they gave you.

🐕 **Be present in the moment** – Just like they lived fully in each day, remind yourself to enjoy the little things.

❋ **Show patience and unconditional love** – Just as they accepted you at your best and worst, do the same for others.

🪶 **Find joy in simple pleasures** – Whether it's feeling the sun on your face, taking a walk, or enjoying a quiet moment, let their spirit remind you that happiness is found in the now.

🐶 **Example:** After losing her dog, Rusty, Emily made a promise to herself: **she would always greet the people she loved with the same excitement and warmth that Rusty greeted her with every day.**

By choosing to live with **the love they embodied,** you allow their spirit to shine through you.

Finding Comfort in the Small Reminders

Even though they are gone, **their presence lingers in the spaces they once filled.** Instead of avoiding these reminders, you can choose to **see them as signs of love rather than loss.**

🐾 **Ways to Find Comfort in Their Memory:**

🔦 **Visit their favorite spot** – Whether it was a sunny windowsill, a cozy blanket, or the foot of your bed, sit there and remember the warmth they brought.

📷 **Keep a special item close** – A collar, a toy, a blanket—these physical reminders can bring comfort rather than sorrow.

🕯 **Create a quiet moment of reflection** – Light a candle, whisper their name, or simply take a deep breath and feel their presence around you.

🐾 **Example:** Mark used to sit on his back porch with his cat, Willow, every morning. After she passed, he continued the ritual—**now with a cup of coffee and a quiet moment of gratitude for her love.**

The reminders don't have to be painful. **They can be sources of comfort, gentle ways to keep their presence alive in your daily life.**

Sharing Their Story: Keeping Their Memory Alive

One of the most beautiful ways to **honor your pet's legacy** is simply by **keeping their story alive.** Speaking their name, reminiscing about their quirks, and sharing memories ensures that **their love continues to exist in the world.**

🐾 **Ways to Share Their Story:**

📖 **Tell friends and family about them** – Share the funny, sweet, and heartwarming moments that made them special.

📝 **Write about them** – Keep a journal, post on social media, or even start a blog about their impact on your life.

🎗 **Create a tribute** – Whether it's a photo album, a scrapbook, or an online memorial, **having a dedicated space to celebrate their life keeps their memory alive.**

💡 **Example:** After losing his dog, Buddy, Jake started telling his young niece bedtime stories about **"a brave and loyal dog named Buddy."** In this way, **Buddy's spirit lived on in the hearts of new generations.**

Keeping their memory alive isn't about **holding onto sadness—it's about ensuring their love never fades.**

Final Thoughts

Your pet's love **didn't end when they left—it continues in the way you live, love, and remember them.**

By **reflecting their kindness, embracing the small reminders, and sharing their story,** you keep their spirit alive every single day.

Because **their love was never meant to be forgotten—it was meant to be carried forward, always.** 🖤

Turning Pain into Purpose

Grief can feel overwhelming, but one of the most powerful ways to heal is to **turn your pain into something meaningful.** The love you shared with your pet doesn't have to stay in the past—it can **inspire kindness, action, and a legacy that continues beyond their time with you.**

By using your experience to support others, advocating for animal welfare, or creating a lasting tribute, you **transform your loss into something that makes a difference.**

Using Your Experience to Support Others

Losing a pet is a unique and deeply personal grief—one that not everyone understands. **But because you have walked this path, you can now be a source of comfort for others who are struggling.**

🐾 **Ways to Help Others Through Their Grief:**

♥ **Listen with empathy** – If a friend or family member loses a pet, offer them the same kindness and understanding you needed.

▢ **Share your story** – Whether through writing, social media, or conversations, letting others know they're not alone can be incredibly healing.

⬤ **Join or create a pet loss support group** – Online forums, local meetups, or social media groups can provide a safe space for others to grieve.

🐶 **Example:** After losing his golden retriever, Max, Daniel started responding to posts in pet loss groups, sharing his experience and offering words of encouragement. **Helping others navigate their grief gave him a sense of purpose and connection.**

Your pain can become **a bridge of understanding for someone else**—a way to remind them that their grief is valid and that they are not alone.

Advocating for Animal Welfare

Another way to honor your pet's legacy is by **helping other animals in need.** Whether through adoption, fostering, volunteering, or raising awareness, your efforts can **turn grief into action.**

🐾 **Ways to Get Involved:**

🏠 **Support shelters and rescues** – Donate supplies, contribute financially, or volunteer your time.

🐕 **Promote adoption** – Share information about pet adoption to help animals find loving homes.

📣 **Raise awareness about pet loss** – Encourage conversations about the importance of acknowledging pet grief and supporting grieving pet owners.

🐾 **Example:** When Mia lost her cat, Luna, she started donating to a local rescue on Luna's adoption anniversary. **Each year, she felt like she was continuing Luna's legacy by helping another cat in need.**

If your pet **changed your life**, imagine how you can pass that love forward to help another.

Creating a Lasting Tribute

Memorializing your pet in a personal way can help **channel grief into a meaningful, lasting legacy.** Whether big or small, creating a tribute ensures that **their love continues to be honored.**

🐾 **Ways to Create a Memorial in Their Name:**

📖 **Start a journal** – Write about their life, their impact on you, and the lessons they taught.

🌿 **Create a physical tribute** – Plant a tree, set up a remembrance corner, or make a custom piece of artwork.

💜 **Dedicate acts of kindness to them** – Leave a donation in their name, help an animal in need, or simply perform small acts of love in their honor.

🐾 **Example:** After losing her dog, Buddy, Rachel decided to bake homemade dog treats and donate them to local shelters. **She called them "Buddy's Treats" and found joy in knowing that his love was still spreading.**

Final Thoughts

Turning pain into purpose **doesn't mean forgetting—it means using love to create something meaningful.** Whether through supporting others, advocating for animals, or creating a tribute, **you are ensuring that their legacy continues.**

Because their love wasn't meant to end—it was meant to **make a difference.** 💜

Embracing the Future While Keeping Their Spirit Alive

Moving forward after losing a beloved pet doesn't mean leaving them behind. **Their love remains with you— woven into your heart, your memories, and the person you've become because of them.** Nothing can take that away.

Grief may change over time, but **love is constant.** It doesn't fade, nor does it disappear—it simply **finds new ways to exist within you.**

Your Love for Them Is Forever

The bond you shared with your pet was deep and unbreakable. **Their absence doesn't mean that love is gone—it means you now carry it differently.**

🐾 **Ways to Keep Their Spirit Close:**

♡ **Say their name.** Keep speaking about them, sharing their stories, and holding them in conversations.

🪶 **Keep a daily reminder.** Whether it's a framed photo, a keepsake, or a small ritual, let their presence remain part of your life.

🐕 **Live with the love they gave you.** Their kindness, patience, and joy can continue through you.

🐶 **Example:** After losing her dog, Toby, Lisa started whispering, *"Goodnight, Toby,"* every night before bed. It was a small but powerful way to remind herself that **he was still with her, always.**

You Deserve to Live a Full, Happy Life

Sometimes, grief makes it hard to imagine joy again. You might even feel guilty at the thought of moving forward. But if your pet could tell you anything, it would be this:

"Be happy. Live fully. Love as deeply as you loved me."

♡ **You are not betraying them by embracing life again.**

♡ **Happiness doesn't erase their memory—it honors it.**

♡ **They would want you to feel the same love, warmth, and comfort you gave them.**

🐾 **Example:** After months of mourning her cat, Whiskers, Emily finally went on a weekend trip with friends. At first, she hesitated, feeling guilty for enjoying herself. But then she remembered **how much Whiskers loved curling up next to her when she was happy— and she realized that finding joy again was a way of honoring him.**

You **deserve to love, laugh, and embrace life**—not despite their memory, but **because of it.**

Their Memory Is Part of Your Story, Not the End of It

Your pet's story doesn't stop at loss. **It continues in every lesson they taught you, every habit they shaped, and every way they changed your heart.**

They are not just a part of your past—**they are a part of you, forever.**

🐾 **How to Carry Their Memory Forward:**

📖 **Write about what they meant to you.** Keep a journal or scrapbook of your favorite moments together.

🐾 **Let their love guide you.** Use the kindness they showed you to be kind to yourself and others.

🌟 **Continue their legacy.** Whether through volunteering, fostering, or simply living with more compassion, let their presence remain part of your journey.

🐾 **Example:** After losing his dog, Buddy, Mark realized that Buddy had taught him patience, joy, and loyalty. **So, instead of closing himself off, he made a promise: to live with the same love Buddy had given him.**

Final Thoughts

Your pet's love **was never meant to end with loss—it was meant to stay with you, shaping your future.**

As you step forward, remember: **They are still with you, in your heart, in your actions, and in the way you carry their love into the world.**

Because their story **is forever a part of yours.** ❤

Your Next Steps—Moving Forward with Love and Peace: A Final Reflection Exercise

Healing from pet loss is not about leaving them behind—it's about **finding ways to carry their love forward while allowing yourself to embrace life again.** Now that you've journeyed through grief, reflection, and healing, it's time to take an important step: **intentionally deciding how you will honor their memory and move forward with love and peace.**

This final reflection exercise will help you recognize what your pet taught you, how you want to keep their legacy alive, and the joyful way you wish to remember them.

1. Write Down Three Things You've Learned Through Your Pet's Passing

Grief has a way of teaching us profound lessons about love, resilience, and the depth of our hearts. Through this experience, what have you learned about yourself, about love, or about life?

🐾 **Some Lessons Your Pet May Have Taught You:**

💜 **Love is unconditional** – They showed you how to love without judgment or expectation.

🦴 **The present moment matters** – They embraced each day with joy, reminding you to do the same.

💜 **Healing takes time, but it happens** – Even in pain, you have found strength you never knew you had.

📝 **Your Reflection:**

1 **What is one lesson your pet's passing has taught you about life?**

2 **How has this experience changed the way you see love or grief?**

3 **In what ways are you stronger now than when your journey of loss began?**

2. List One Way You Will Honor Their Legacy Moving Forward

Keeping their memory alive can be as simple as **continuing a small tradition in their name** or as significant as **dedicating time to helping other animals.** The way you honor them should be **personal and meaningful to you.**

🐾 **Ways to Honor Their Legacy:**

🌿 **Plant a tree or flowers in their favorite spot** – A living tribute that grows just like your love.

🐕 **Donate or volunteer at a shelter** – Give back to animals in need, just as your pet gave love to you.

📖 **Start a journal or blog about them** – Keep their memory alive by writing about the lessons they taught you.

🐾 **Celebrate them on special dates** – Light a candle, take a walk, or do something in their honor.

📝 **Your Reflection:**

💜 **What is one meaningful way you will honor their memory moving forward?**

🐾 **Example:** After losing her cat, Oliver, Sarah decided to donate to a cat rescue every year on the anniversary of his adoption, ensuring that **his love continued to help others.**

3. Describe How You Want to Remember Them: A Joyful Memory to Carry with You

Instead of letting grief define their memory, choose a **moment of pure joy** that represents their spirit. When you think of them, let **this memory bring a smile to your face instead of just sadness.**

🐾 **How to Choose a Memory:**

💜 **Think of a moment that captures their personality** – A funny habit, a silly quirk, or a heartwarming moment.

💜 **Pick a memory that brings warmth, not pain** – One that reminds you of how much love you shared.

💜 **Let this be your anchor** – Whenever sadness creeps in, return to this memory as a source of comfort.

📝 **Your Reflection:**

🐾 **What is the happiest or most comforting memory you have of your pet?**

🐾 **When you think of them, what moment will bring a smile to your face?**

Example: Every time Jake thinks of his dog, Buddy, he remembers how Buddy would greet him at the door, tail wagging wildly, no matter how long he had been gone. **That's the memory he chooses to hold onto—the pure, unconditional love that will always be with him.**

Final Thoughts

Your pet's passing has changed you, but **it hasn't taken away the love they left behind.** You've learned valuable lessons from them, and their presence will continue to shape your life in meaningful ways.

By reflecting on their impact, choosing a way to honor them, and holding onto a joyful memory, **you are moving forward—not away from them, but with them in your heart.**

Because love doesn't end. **It simply takes new forms.**

Permission to Feel Joy Again

Grief can sometimes make joy feel out of reach. Even when healing begins, a lingering sense of guilt may whisper that moving forward means leaving your pet behind. But **healing doesn't mean forgetting—it means learning to carry love in a new way.**

You are not betraying them by finding happiness again. **In fact, joy is one of the greatest ways to honor their memory.**

Healing Doesn't Mean Forgetting – Let Go of Any Lingering Guilt

It's natural to feel guilty when you start to feel lighter. The first time you smile without pain, the first time you enjoy a walk that once felt empty, or the first time you consider welcoming another pet into your life—**these moments can bring an unexpected wave of guilt.**

But here's the truth: **Feeling joy again doesn't mean you've forgotten them. It means their love is still with you, shaping the way you live.**

🐾 **Things to Remind Yourself When Guilt Creeps In:**

🤍 **Your pet would never want you to stay in pain.** They gave you unconditional love—**they would want the same for you now.**

🐾 **Letting go of sorrow doesn't mean letting go of love.** Their memory is part of you forever, no matter how much happiness returns.

🐶 **Your life still holds meaning and joy.** Just as they enriched your days, you deserve to keep living fully.

🐾 **Example:** After losing her dog, Bailey, Emma felt guilty the first time she went on a morning walk and enjoyed it. But then she realized: **Bailey loved those walks, and she could still carry that joy forward in his honor.**

You are **not moving on from them—you are moving forward with them.**

It's Okay to Love Another Pet Someday – Love Is Infinite

Some pet owners fear that adopting another animal is a form of replacement, but **love doesn't work that way.** Your heart is not limited in its ability to love—**it only expands.**

Welcoming another pet, when you are ready, doesn't mean you are erasing your past pet's memory. **It means you are honoring the love they gave you by sharing it with another animal in need.**

🐾 **When Considering Another Pet, Ask Yourself:**

💜 **Am I welcoming them with an open heart, not as a replacement but as a new beginning?**

🤍 **Does the thought of companionship bring warmth, rather than just sadness?**

🍃 **Am I ready to offer love again, knowing that each pet is unique and special in their own way?**

🐾 **Example:** After grieving her cat, Milo, for nearly a year, Sarah felt drawn to a rescue shelter. She knew no cat could ever replace Milo, but when she met a quiet, shy kitten in need of a home, she felt her heart open again—not as a replacement, but as a continuation of the love Milo had shown her.

If and when you feel ready, **know that opening your heart again is not a betrayal—it is a testament to the love your pet taught you.**

You Are Allowed to Embrace Happiness Again – This Is What They Would Want for You

If your pet could tell you anything, it would be this:

🐾 *"Be happy. Love again. Live your life fully—just like you did with me."*

They didn't spend their days dwelling in sadness, and they wouldn't want that for you either. **They lived in the moment, found joy in the simplest things, and loved without hesitation.**

🐾 **Ways to Welcome Joy Back Into Your Life:**

⚙ **Find happiness in the small things.** Take walks, laugh, enjoy the sun—**the same way they did.**

♥ **Celebrate their life rather than focus on their passing.** Let their memory bring warmth instead of only sorrow.

🐾 **Give yourself permission to love again.** Whether through deepening relationships, opening your heart to a new pet, or simply embracing each day with gratitude, **joy is not a betrayal—it is a continuation of the love they left behind.**

🐾 **Example:** Mark had been hesitant to laugh, enjoy a movie, or go out with friends after losing his dog, Duke. But one day, he realized that **Duke would have wanted him to be happy.** Instead of feeling guilty for laughing, he let himself feel grateful—for all the love, the memories, and the time they shared.

Final Thoughts

Healing doesn't mean forgetting. Loving again doesn't mean replacing. **And finding joy again doesn't mean losing what you had.**

You are allowed to smile, to laugh, to love again—**because that is what your pet would want for you.** 🖤

A Heartfelt Closing Message

> *"Grief may change you, but it doesn't have to break you. The love you shared with your pet is a gift that will last a lifetime. As you move forward, carry that love with you—not as a burden, but as a light. Your pet will always be a part of your heart, and through your actions, their spirit will continue to shine. Let love, not loss, guide your journey ahead."*

Final Call to Action: Moving Forward with Love and Purpose

You have walked the path of grief, honored the love you shared, and taken steps toward healing. **Now, it's time to move forward—not by letting go, but by carrying their love with you.**

Your pet's memory is a gift—one that can continue to **shape, inspire, and comfort you** for years to come. Taking **intentional steps** will help you integrate their love into your life in a way that brings you **peace, joy, and connection.**

📌 Final Steps to Take Right Now:

✅ **Complete the reflection exercise** – Write down:

1. Three things your pet's passing has taught you.

2. One way you will honor their legacy moving forward.

3. A joyful memory of them that you will carry with you.

Taking a moment to reflect will **cement your healing journey** and remind you that **their love lives on in you.**

✅ **Create a small, daily ritual to honor their memory.**

- Light a candle, whisper their name, or spend a moment in their favorite spot.

- Carry a keepsake, write in a gratitude journal, or take a mindful walk in their honor.

- Choose something that **brings you comfort** and makes their presence feel close.

✅ **Stay connected to a community of support.**

Grief is easier when shared. Whether through **friends, family, online support groups, or local pet loss communities,** connecting with others who understand can help ease the burden.

🐾 **You don't have to go through this alone. Love and support are always within reach.**

Final Thoughts

Your pet's story doesn't end here. **It continues with you, in your heart, in your actions, and in the way you choose to live.**

Carry their love forward, embrace the happiness they would have wanted for you, and know that **they will always be a part of your journey.**

Because love, once given, **never fades—it lives on, in you.** ♥

Thank You for Choosing This Book

Dear Reader,

From the bottom of my heart, **thank you** for choosing this book and for allowing me to walk alongside you on this deeply personal journey. Losing a beloved pet is one of the hardest experiences we face, but the love they gave us never truly leaves. I hope that through these pages, you have found **comfort, understanding, and a path forward that honors both your grief and the unbreakable bond you shared.**

If this book has helped you in any way, I would truly appreciate it if you could **leave a review** on the site where you purchased it (such as Amazon). Your words not only help others who are going through the same pain, but they also allow this book to reach more people who need guidance and support.

I wish you **peace, healing, and love** as you continue forward. May your pet's memory always bring you warmth, and may you find ways to carry their spirit with you in joy.

You are never alone in this journey, and their love will always be a part of you. 🖤

> *"Don't Cry Because It's Over, Smile Because It Happened."*
> *Dr. Seuss*

With gratitude, love and compassion,

Andre St Pierre

References

American Veterinary Medical Association. (n.d.). *Pet loss support and grief resources.* Retrieved from https://www.avma.org/resources-tools/pet-owners/pet-loss

Archer, J. (1997). *Why do people love their pets?* Evolution and Human Behavior, 18(4), 237-259.

Association for Pet Loss and Bereavement. (n.d.). *Understanding pet loss grief.* Retrieved from https://www.aplb.org/grief/

Becker, M. (2018). *The healing power of pets: Harnessing the amazing ability of pets to make and keep people happy and healthy.* Hachette Books.

Cornell University College of Veterinary Medicine. (2022). *Anticipatory grief and coping with pet loss.* Retrieved from https://www.vet.cornell.edu/petloss

Fine, A. H. (2019). *Handbook on animal-assisted therapy: Foundations and guidelines for animal-assisted interventions* (5th ed.). Academic Press.

Fitzpatrick, N. (2021). *How animals saved my life: Being the supervet.* Trapeze.

Frommer, S. S., & Arguello, A. P. (2006). *Pet loss and human bereavement.* Routledge.

Harvard Health Publishing. (2021). *Why losing a pet can feel as painful as losing a person.* Retrieved from https://www.health.harvard.edu/blog/pet-loss-grief

Kübler-Ross, E., & Kessler, D. (2005). *On grief and grieving: Finding the meaning of grief through the five stages of loss.* Scribner.

Mayo Clinic. (2023). *Coping with grief after pet loss.* Retrieved from https://www.mayoclinic.org/healthy-lifestyle/stress-management/in-depth/grief/art-20047301

Psychology Today. (2020). *The psychology of pet loss.* Retrieved from https://www.psychologytoday.com/us/blog/animal-emotions/202010/the-psychology-pet-loss

Rainbow Bridge Pet Loss Grief Center. (n.d.). *Healing from pet loss: Understanding grief and finding support.* Retrieved from https://www.rainbowsbridge.com/grief_support.htm

Sife, W. (2014). *The loss of a pet: A guide to coping with the grieving process when a pet dies* (4th ed.). Howell Book House.

Tufts University Cummings School of Veterinary Medicine. (2022). *Helping children cope with pet loss.* Retrieved from https://vet.tufts.edu/petloss

Walfish, S. (2011). *Pet loss counseling: Helping our clients through the grief, loss, and healing process.* Professional Resource Press.